Who Am I in Christ?

I.D.

Natalie Durso

journey**forth**®

Greenville, South Carolina

I.D.—Who Am I in Christ?
Natalie Durso

Design by Craig Oesterling
Page layout by Michael Boone

© 2015 by BJU Press
Greenville, South Carolina 29614
JourneyForth Books is a division of BJU Press.

Printed in the United States of America

ISBN 978-1-60682-993-6

15   14   13   12   11   10   9   8   7   6   5   4   3   2   1

For Michael,
whose encouragement and example
prompted me to find my security in Christ
long before I ever thought of writing about it.

CONTENTS

Introduction

(Please don't skip the intro like I'm always tempted to do!)

I made an interesting discovery a few weeks ago. I found my high school diary in a box of old stuff crammed under my bed. I had an entertaining time reading through all the entries my teenage self had hurriedly and sloppily recorded with my multicolored gel pens. Along with noticing that I was definitely a drama queen, I picked up on another theme. All throughout my high school years, I was always trying to answer these questions:

Who am I?

Where do I fit in?

What do people think about me?

Do they like who I am?

Back up with me to a few months before I rediscovered my diary. As I write this, I am a twenty-six-year-old woman, happily married for almost four years to the man of my dreams. I completed two years of teaching communications to college students, and I am now working in a demanding job as a legal assistant and serving as a sponsor to the teens in our church youth group. You would think that I would have the question "Who am I?" completely answered by now, and maybe I should. But after a series of public incidents in which I felt completely rejected by people around me and night after night of going home and tearfully asking my husband if anyone besides him actually liked me, I decided I needed to do something about all my insecurities.

Our culture offers a million different solutions to my problem, a problem they would probably call low self-esteem. There are programs geared toward helping people of all ages to discover themselves and find their self-worth. Positive thinking about yourself and your abilities is encouraged. You are expected to love yourself and express yourself and be yourself. Yet on the other hand, girls are barraged daily by fashions, celebrities, role models, and advertisements that exalt the perfect body, face, and personality. All of this can't help but push most of us to despair of ever reaching the unattainable standard of perfection. Friends, popularity, good looks, or talent are often viewed as the way to measure the success of a person, and so a young woman starts comparing herself with those around her to see how she measures up. All the while, she is constantly trying to decide who she wants to be and establish how she wants people to perceive her. Whew! That's just too much for a poor girl to handle.

As a Christian, I knew that the things the world proposed as solutions to my insecurity crisis would never fix my problem. The only true, lasting solutions come from God and His Word, and I knew that's where I needed to go. I just wasn't exactly sure where to start. The Bible doesn't have a self-help index or three easy steps for solving my how-to-get-over-my-desire-to-be-universally-liked-and-appreciated-for-who-I-am problem. I already knew my insecurities revealed how proud I was and that I was thinking about me all the time. I wanted to discover, from the Bible, who God says that I am and should be. So I began a study that I simply called "Who Am I?" (WAI? for short).

I started in Romans and began to read every verse, searching for clues as to who God says I am or who He wants me to be. Next to each pertinent verse, I wrote *WAI?* in the margin and then the principle I found in that verse—for example: "WAI? I'm loved by God no matter what." But it didn't take me long in my study to realize that my title was incomplete. I was trying to discover something about myself without taking into account the most important, defining factor in my life. What makes me who I am? What defines, or should define, how I live each day of my life? What could eliminate my tendency to live to please people and to worry about what they think of me? The key concept I needed to look for in my study was "Who Am I . . . *in Christ?*" Christ is the difference from the self-discovery journeys the world would encourage me to take. I am defined by Christ and what He has done for me. So my study about how to correct my me-centered focus turns out to not be about me at all. Shocking, right? The entire focus is on Christ.

Consider some of the following situations:

You walk into a room and instantly start sizing up people around you to see how you compare or how you can fit in.

You want desperately to be popular, to have a lot of friends, and to receive attention from more people at school and church.

You are always self-conscious about the way you look, and you thrive on compliments on your outfit, hair, or accomplishments.

You think your opinions or ideas should be taken seriously, but you are hesitant to share them for fear other people won't like them.

You are mopey, moody, or angry after being treated poorly by others.

You're jealous of someone else's looks, personality, or performance.

You feel left out or pushed aside by certain groups of people, and you dwell on this fact for long periods of time, trying to figure out how you can fit in with them.

You cave in to peer pressure around you and do things you shouldn't do so you'll be accepted.

Or consider these situations:

You gloat about your accomplishments, talents, popularity, or appearance.

You enjoy the constant spotlight and always seek ways to divert attention back to yourself.

You participate in gossip or use sarcasm to make yourself look better or to make people think you're funny.

You thrust your opinions or ideas forward as the best way or only way to do something.

You voice your two cents without hesitating, even if it's not an appropriate time or situation for you to do so.

You serve so that people will notice you and think you're a good person.

You flirt to attract attention and feel special.

You create peer-pressure situations and try to get people to follow you.

I honestly believe that everyone struggles with insecurity in one form or another; we just deal with it in different ways. The first group of examples listed above is a category I'm calling the Pleasers. These are people who are insecure and therefore try to change who they are depending on who they're with at the time. A Pleaser will desperately seek common ground with others, try to buy affection, try to blend in with the crowd, and will always walk away from an interaction with people with her mood either enhanced or destroyed based on her performance that day. Let me just go ahead and tell you: I'm a Pleaser.

The second group of examples is what I call the Confidents. These people will not come across as insecure at all on the outside. A Confident will approach every situation and person, assuming that she's already liked. She pushes her personality, looks, opinions, or abilities to the forefront. She may seem totally comfortable with who she is. A Confident is the person to whom a Pleaser looks to see how to behave. For years, I thought the Confidents in my life had it all together and that I needed to try to be like them. More recently, however, I've learned that often a Confident is just as insecure as a Pleaser, but she has found that the way to make life go her way is to act like she doesn't care what people think of her. She will push her personality forward, acting like she's got it all together, and people believe it. Deep inside, though, she just wants people to like her, and her outward show is the way to gain that attention.

Neither of those ways of handling insecurities is correct. Picture this instead: A girl walks into a room full of people. She is thinking about these people and how she can serve them, minister to them, and best glorify God through her interactions with them. When she walks away from an evening where she doesn't feel like she was included or knows someone else was more popular than she was, she doesn't dwell on it because that's not what's most important to her. She doesn't compare herself with others, compete with others, seek the favor of others, or change her actions based on how others treat her. She knows what's important, and she doesn't base her success on how many compliments she got or how many friends she has. She is confident in who the Bible says she is, which means that she is humble. She is defined by Christ and Christ alone.

I was fourteen years old when my sister-in-law introduced me to *Strong's Exhaustive Concordance of the Bible*, a book that probably weighed more than I did at the time. I've been hooked on it ever since. Now all of these resources are online, although I sometimes still enjoy hauling out my monster *Strong's* and manually searching for the words. I'm pretty positive that if you're capable of reading this, you're capable of locating the Greek words using a concordance like *Strong's* or online Bible study resources or software.[1] In the word study sections I will include a number in parentheses that refers to the word number in *Strong's*. You can find that word by number in *Strong's* to learn the meaning(s) of the word in the original language. Sure, I could tell you, "In the Greek, this word means _____," and I will do that sometimes. However, I've discovered that I actually learn and remember things better when I'm the one that has to do the digging, not when someone does it for me. You can listen to a powerful and inspiring sermon, but the only way that passage of Scripture will come alive and actually become a part of your life is when you take the time (as the preacher did) to study it for yourself and to allow the Lord to illumine your heart to His truth. I've seen this happen in my own life often enough that I'm absolutely not going to cheat you out of the opportunity to dig into God's Word and discover His treasures for yourself.

My goal is to make this study challenging but not discouragingly hard. If you feel like some of the material is too difficult for you, I encourage you to ask someone you respect to help you get started on some of the new study methods, or simply walk away from that chapter and come back to it the next day. Let's face it, sometimes we just have brain-dead days. If you come back to a passage after a rest from it and re-approach it with a prayer that the Lord will open your eyes, you may have very different results. He wants to show Himself to you. Just don't give up. Don't try to do a whole chapter in a day. Go at your own pace; keep digging, and the Lord will reward your desire. I'm going to be with you every step of the way, sharing with you what I'm learning because, remember, this study was originally just for me. I won't ask you to share something that I'm not prepared to share myself. So let's jump in and figure out together how we're defined by Christ!

—Natalie

SECTION 1
Who Am I in Christ in Relation to Sin?

1
Hopeless Without Him

What a great way to start, right? Bet you didn't wake up this morning expecting someone to tell you that life is hopeless. Trust me, the encouragement is coming by the truckloads, but before we get there, we have to start with where we came from, and it's not pretty. But stay with me.

I love reading. I'm a big fan of the classics written by the likes of Charles Dickens, Jane Austen, the Brontës, C. S. Lewis, Elizabeth Gaskell, J. R. R. Tolkien, and . . . You get the idea. As much as most of us hate conflict, you really can't have a good story without it. If the hero and heroine just coast through the book with no problems, no internal struggles, no battles, and no bad guys, you have a pretty boring read on your hands. A good story usually turns incredibly hopeless before the triumph comes. It looks like Elizabeth Bennet and Mr. Darcy will never get together. It appears that Frodo will never make it to Mount Doom to destroy the Ring before all of Middle Earth is destroyed. It seems like the White Witch will conquer all of Narnia since she successfully killed Aslan. You're sure Scrooge used up his last chance and will die alone and friendless because of his selfish life. These are the chapters that come right before the happy ending and have us biting our nails as we read, wondering how this mess can possibly be resolved in a satisfactory way.

That's what this chapter is: the horrible, hopeless chapter. But without this chapter, we really couldn't fully appreciate the chapters that come after it. Without the hero of the story being brought to the end of himself and thinking that everything is lost, we wouldn't really be excited about his happily ever after.

I don't want to trivialize the salvation story by likening it to a novel but rather urge you to keep reading after this chapter, because even though this isn't a fun one, they won't all be like this. The resolution to the hopelessness is coming later, but first let's slog through the conflict chapter.

Whether you're a Confident or a Pleaser, both attitudes focus on one person: yourself. Both attitudes have the same root: pride. We all think of ourselves far too often and estimate our value as far too high. The best way to kill pride is to drown it with a good dose of the truth. So in this chapter we need to examine who we are without Christ.

Many of you probably know Romans 3:23 by heart: "For all have sinned, and come short of the glory of God." We know that we're sinners, but we view that fact pretty casually. We don't realize all that this reveals about who we are—or, rather, who we were before salvation.

READ ALL ABOUT IT

In this section, I'm going to write out some verses for you to work through.

1. Read each verse one time and <u>underline</u> any words that describe your condition without God. There are many different ones.

2. Go through each verse a second time and circle any specific sins that you find.

3. Go through a third time and put a star (☆) next to any consequences of sin.

And even as they did not like to retain God in their knowledge, God gave them over to a reprobate mind, to do those things which are not convenient; being filled with all unrighteousness, fornication, wickedness, covetousness, maliciousness; full of envy, murder, debate, deceit, malignity; whisperers, backbiters, haters of God, despiteful, proud, boasters, inventors of evil things, disobedient to parents, without understanding, covenantbreakers, without natural affection, implacable, unmerciful: who knowing the judgment of God, that they which commit such things are worthy of death, not only do the same, but have pleasure in them that do them. Therefore thou art inexcusable, O man, whosoever thou art that judgest: for wherein thou judgest another, thou condemnest thyself; for thou that judgest doest the same things. (Romans 1:28–2:1)

For when we were yet without strength, in due time Christ died for the ungodly. For scarcely for a righteous man will one die: yet peradventure for a good man some would even dare to die. But God commendeth his love toward us, in that, while we were yet sinners, Christ died for us. (Romans 5:6–8)

For the wages of sin is death. (Romans 6:23)

For I know that in me (that is, in my flesh,) dwelleth no good thing: for to will is present with me; but how to perform that which is good I find not. For the good that I would I do not: but the evil which I would not, that I do. . . . O wretched man that I am! who shall deliver me from the body of this death? (Romans 7:18, 19, and 24)

And you hath he quickened, who were dead in trespasses and sins; wherein in time past ye walked according to the course of this world, according to the prince of the power of the air, the spirit that now worketh in the children of disobedience: among whom also we all had our conversation in times past in the lusts of our flesh, fulfilling the desires of the flesh and of the mind; and were by nature the children of wrath, even as others. . . . Even when we were dead in sins . . . that at that time ye were without Christ, being aliens from the commonwealth of Israel, and strangers from the covenants of promise, having no hope, and without God in the world. (Ephesians 2:1–3, 5, and 12)

And you, that were sometime alienated and enemies in your mind by wicked works, yet now hath he reconciled. (Colossians 1:21)

And you, being dead in your sins and the uncircumcision of your flesh, hath he quickened together with him, having forgiven you all trespasses. (Colossians 2:13)

What's It Mean?

Write out the negative words you found in those verses that describe who you are without God, so you can see them all in one place.

_____

_____

Yuck! This paints a pretty hopeless picture of you, doesn't it? However, if you were reading those verses in your Bible instead of seeing them written out, you'd notice something else. I actually dissected those verses and only gave you bits and pieces. I cut out the good news and the answer to the rest of our question: Who am I . . . *in Christ?* We don't have to wallow in all of those ugly words because, while they display one aspect of who we are, they don't complete the picture for those of us with Christ in our life!

So why did I make you study all that miserable stuff about your condition before salvation? Because we can't fully appreciate who we are in Christ until we recognize who we are *without* Christ. Like I said earlier, we're all naturally very proud. There isn't a single Christian who doesn't have to fight pride on a daily basis. I don't like to focus on things I've done wrong. I don't naturally like to admit that I need help. I don't enjoy it when someone else is perceived as being better at something than I am.

I need to be reminded every day that without Christ I am nothing. I am dead in my sins and separated from God. I can do no good thing. I've fallen short; I've missed the mark; I have no hope . . . *without Christ.* Please let this sink in. Think about it for more than just the time it takes to read that sentence. Because of Christ, all of those disgusting, hopeless descriptions of you are part of your past. Meditating on who you were before salvation is a surefire way to kill pride.

What's It Mean to You?

Take a few minutes to record at least five ways that you have already fallen short of God's standard (that is, ways you've sinned), just today. Even if you just woke up, you probably can already find this many. If you're not used to actively looking for sin in your life, this might be a tough assignment, but don't give yourself a break. Really examine each thought and action. (Maybe you stayed in bed so long that you didn't have much time to spend with God or you gossiped about someone or you had a proud thought or . . .)

1. _____

2. _____

3. _____

4. _____

5. _____

And that list is just today, maybe even just a few hours of today! Now I want you to take this exercise one step further. Find a specific command in God's Word that demonstrates that the sins you wrote down *are* actually sins. In other words, find a verse that tells you what part of God's perfect standard (zero tolerance for sin!) you have violated by your thoughts or actions.

I did this exercise too, so I'll give you an example. One of the things on my list was that I spent too long getting going this morning, wasted time on the computer, and watched TV instead of working on writing this. Those things aren't necessarily sins, but I know that the amount of time I spent on each of them was a sin *for me* because of Ephesians 5:16, which says I should focus on "redeeming [rescuing from being lost] the time, because the days are evil." I directly disobeyed God's command for me to make the most of my time.

Now you try. For each number above, find a command in Scripture that you violated and write the reference below. Maybe you had a thought about God or someone else that didn't match up with Philippians 4:8 or maybe you broke one of the Ten Commandments found in Exodus 20. You can use a concordance to find the exact verses you're looking for.

1. _____

2. _____

3. _____

4. _____

5. _____

So just today, you've broken five commands, straight from God's mouth (and probably a lot more than five, if you're honest!). Now think about how many years you've been alive and all of the sinful thoughts and actions that have been crammed into each minute of each day of each year. Where does that leave you? You are stuck in Romans 3:23: "For (insert your name) [has] sinned and come[s] short [very short!] of the glory of God." If Christ hadn't intervened in your life and saved you, you would be drowning in all of those sins. In the next chapter, we're going to study the marvelous work Christ did in your life if you're a Christian, but for now, just think of where you'd be if He hadn't saved you.

Picture This

If you're still not convinced that the sins you wrote down are so terrible, check out what Jerry Bridges says in his book *Respectable Sins*.

> Sin is sin. Even those sins that I call "the acceptable sins of the saints"—those sins that we tolerate in our lives—are serious in God's eyes. Our religious pride, our critical attitudes, our unkind speech about others, our impatience and anger, even our anxiety . . . all of these are serious in the sight of God."[1]

And in another section he concludes,

> Whether it is large or small in our eyes, it is heinous in the sight of God. God forgives our sin because of the shed blood of Christ, but He does not tolerate it. Instead, every sin that we commit, even the subtle sin that we don't even think about, was laid upon Christ as He bore the curse of God in our place. And herein lies chiefly the malignancy [like cancer] of sin. Christ suffered because of our sins.[2]

Wow! That puts our *little* sins into perspective! *Every* sin is responsible for separating us from God before we were saved, and *every* sin made it necessary for Christ to die on the cross for us.

This is truly a defining aspect of who you are. Even after salvation, your sin nature is still present. We have to be convinced of the depth of our wickedness to maintain the correct view of who we are. The world tells us to be confident in ourselves, but I'm not seeing a whole lot to be confident in from those descriptions of us up there, are you?

WRAP IT UP

Try not to think, "Sure, I guess I'm a sinner," like it's some far-off, hazy concept that doesn't really affect you now that you're saved. Think about it more like this:

- Before Christ you were dead in your sin—a corpse with absolutely no spiritual life.
- Before Christ you were separated from God and had no share in His promised blessings.
- Before Christ you were God's enemy, actively at war with Him through your sin.
- Before Christ you had absolutely no hope and nothing to look forward to, except hell.
- Before Christ you were without God in every area of your life.
- Before Christ you were ungodly, weak, and sinful, and there was *nothing* good about you.

These statements about you as a lost sinner define who you were before Christ was in your life, and this should affect how you view yourself as a saved person every day. It doesn't matter how pretty you are, how sparkling your personality is, what leadership positions you have, how talented, smart, popular, or outgoing you are—you cannot possess true security outside of Christ.

[**DEFINING TRUTH:**
You can't find any security in
yourself.

What should your response be to the knowledge of how sinful you are?

_____

_____

In what ways do you tend to minimize the seriousness of your sin now that you're a Christian?

How will remembering all those words that described you before Christ came into your life help you kill pride in your life now?

Let's make it personal to you. If you tend to be a Confident and draw attention to yourself, your ideas, and your talents, what one truth from this lesson will help you to guard against your form of pride?

If you're a Pleaser, and you always worry about what other people think of you, how you can fit in, and what will please them, what one truth from this lesson will help you fight your form of pride?

I'm now pressing the pause button. Consider yourself paused.

Before you answer any more questions, please go to Appendix 1 on page 166 in the back of the book to read about putting off and putting on. Please read that section completely. We're going to use the information you find there at the end of each chapter, so please don't skip it, or you'll be super confused. Off you go.

Did you read it? No cheating. Answer the questions below based on the **Put Off, Renew, Put On** model you read about.

Think about this lesson and examine your life. Maybe the Lord convicted you about a specific sin you've been struggling with lately. Maybe you're realizing that sin is serious and you've had a casual attitude toward the very sin that put Christ on the cross for you. Or maybe you need to confess those five sins you listed on page 7 in this lesson today. Whatever the case may be, record what you need to work on below. Confessing isn't just writing something down. Take these sin struggles to God and seek His help to rid your life of them!

PUT OFF

1. Confess it and get rid of it

Who besides God have you affected with your sin, and whose forgiveness do you need to ask?

_____

_____

2. Deal with it

When will you go to the person to ask forgiveness, and what will you say?

_____

_____

3. Cut it out

What specific things do you need to remove from your life to make it harder for you to be tempted by this sin?

_____

_____

RENEW YOUR MIND

1. Memorize it

Write out the verse that you plan to memorize.

_____

_____

_____

2. Meditate on it

Please go to Appendix 2 on page 173 in the back of the book to read about ways to meditate. How will this passage renew your mind?

_____

_____

PUT ON

1. Swap it

With what godly thoughts and actions do you need to replace your old sinful thoughts and actions?

_____

_____

2. Check up on it

Who can keep you accountable about your sin struggles? When will you talk to this person about helping you?

_____

2 Saved and Redeemed

ere's where we venture into exciting territory. This is the resolution to the conflict we looked at in the last chapter. The truths in the next two chapters have been the most defining for me in my whole WAI? study. In the last chapter we focused on who we would be without Christ in our lives, and the answer was that we'd be living a life completely dead to God and at war with Him. In this section we're talking about who we are in Christ in relation to our sin. I told you there'd be good news coming, so let's dive into it now.

READ ALL ABOUT IT

Read each of the following verses, and in the space provided, write in your own words the truth you discover about who you are because of Christ. If you don't fully understand some of these words, don't worry; we're going to talk about them in more depth later. (But feel free to get super excited about the ones you understand at first glance!) There may be more than one description in a verse. I'll do the first one for you, just to give you a jump-start.

Being justified freely by his grace through the redemption that is in Christ Jesus. (Romans 3:24)

Remember that Romans 3:23 comes right before, and this is finishing the thought about us as sinners who are now saved. So . . .

Who am I? I am

justified and redeemed from my sin because Jesus died for me!

Therefore being justified by faith, we have peace with God through our Lord Jesus Christ: by whom also we have access by faith into this grace wherein we stand, and rejoice in hope of the glory of God. . . . Much more then, being now justified by his blood, we shall be saved from wrath through him. (Romans 5:1, 2, and 9)

Who am I? I am

Likewise reckon ye also yourselves to be dead indeed unto sin, but alive unto God through Jesus Christ our Lord. (Romans 6:11)

Who am I? I am

I get completely overwhelmed every time I read all of the amazing truths stuffed into Ephesians 1 and 2, but I'll try to just give you a few verses to keep the *overwhelming-ness* to a minimum. Feel free to find more of your own "Who Am I's?" later. You will be in awe—guaranteed!

In whom we have redemption through his blood, the forgiveness of sins, according to the riches of his grace. (Ephesians 1:7)

Who am I? I am

And you hath he quickened, who were dead in trespasses and sins; . . . But God, who is rich in mercy, for his great love wherewith he loved us, even when we were dead in sins, hath quickened us together with Christ, (by grace ye are saved). (Ephesians 2:1, 4, 5)

Who am I? I am

For by grace are ye saved through faith; and that not of yourselves: it is the gift of God: not of works, lest any man should boast. (Ephesians 2:8–9)

Who am I? I am

And you, being dead in your sins and the uncircumcision of your flesh, hath he quickened together with him, having forgiven you all trespasses; Blotting out the handwriting of ordinances that was against us, which was contrary to us, and took it out of the way, nailing it to his cross. (Colossians 2:13, 14)

Who am I? I am

Even though you might have heard the words you wrote down most of your life, a few of them might not mean very much to you. So let's get digging and find out what they mean and why they're so exciting!

What's It Mean?

In this chapter, we'll study *saved* and *redeemed*. Let's start with *saved*.

For by grace are ye saved through faith; and that not of your-selves: it is the gift of God: not of works, lest any man should boast. (Ephesians 2:8–9)

Look up the word *saved* in *Strong's Concordance* and write the definitions you find.

saved (4982)

_____

_____

We looked at our sin condition last lesson and established what we needed to be saved *from*.

What's It Mean to You?

Christians toss around the word *saved* a lot, but have you ever thought of it as meaning rescued? We were on the fast track to death and destruction in hell. Read this excerpt from Jonathan Edwards's sermon, "Sinners in the Hands of an Angry God," which describes hell. Think about yourself and only yourself whenever he says the word *you*. Ignore the old-timey language, and focus on the vivid picture he paints.

That world of misery, that lake of burning brimstone, is extended abroad under you. There is the dreadful pit of the glowing flames of the wrath of God; there is hell's wide gaping mouth open; and you have nothing to stand upon, nor any thing to take hold of; there is nothing between you and hell but the air; it is only the power and mere pleasure of God that holds you up. . . . Your wickedness makes you as it were heavy as lead, and to tend downwards with great weight and pressure towards hell; and if God should let you go, you would immediately sink and swiftly descend and plunge into the bottomless gulf, and your healthy constitu-tion, and your own care and prudence, and best contriv-ance, and all your righteousness, would have no more influence to uphold you and keep you out of hell, than a spider's web would have to stop a falling rock. Were it not for the sovereign pleasure of God, the earth would not bear you one moment.[1]

Wow! Do you feel the urgency and the hopelessness of sinners' condition in his words? This was you before you were . . . *saved*. Sometimes we don't think of the word *saved* as being literally rescued.

When you tell someone that God saved you, do you really think about what that means? It's often just a casual state of being for a Christian: yeah, I'm *saved*; my parents are *saved*; my friends are *saved* too. We're supposed to tell other people how to *get saved*. Yawn. When someone asks for our salvation testimony, we often rattle off in monotone the time, the place, how old we were, what we said, when we doubted, and how we stopped doubting . . . without even once being overwhelmed by what salvation means!

Picture This

Imagine yourself stuck on the twentieth story of a burning building with no hope of getting out. The flames are getting higher and hotter, and all of the exits are blocked. No one is around to hear you screaming for help. You're running out of air and hope. Just as you're about to gasp your last breath, a strong, courageous firefighter breaks down the fiery door and carries you to safety.

How would you retell that story to your friends? Would you slouch down and fold your arms, sound bored or embarrassed? Would you try to get the story over with as quickly as possible, gloss over the involvement of the brave firefighter, and just focus on the facts with no emotion in your voice?

Um, I don't think so.

This would be your go-to story to tell for the rest of your life! You would be animated, telling everyone you met, expounding on every detail, focusing on how bad the fire was, how desperate you were to get out, how hopeless it seemed, praising the firefighter, overflowing with emotion and thanks for the one who . . . *saved* you.

This is the same idea, but to a far lesser degree compared to your soul's salvation. The firefighter saved your physical body from a horrible death. What are some of the things Christ rescued you from?

_____

_____

The rest of Ephesians 2:8–9 tells us how we were saved. It's all about Christ, His death on the cross, and His resurrection. According to those verses, what has no effect on our salvation whatsoever?

_____

What is one reason God designed His salvation plan that way? (See the last few words of verse 9.)

_____

Salvation has everything to do with God's *grace*. Some definitions you might have heard for *grace* are "God's unmerited favor"; "God giving us what we don't deserve"; "God's riches at Christ's expense." All of those are very good and correct definitions, but I'm going to give you one found in *Strong's Dictionary* because it's my favorite definition of grace ever. *Grace* (5485) is "the divine influence on the heart and its reflection in the life." This definition is true of saving grace as well as of God's grace that sustains us all through the rest of our lives. He has given us His overabundant grace for all situations in life. When God influences our hearts, it's only then that we can live as Christians should live.

His grace is active in our salvation because the Holy Spirit convicts us of our need for a Savior (influencing our hearts); and when we turn to Him in repentance (His reflection on our lives), He will save us. It's only by His grace that He offered salvation to helpless sinners like us.

Do you ever live like your salvation is dependent on how many good things you do? If we could do enough good things to earn salvation, Christ wouldn't have had to come and die for us. We would've just lived our lives feverishly trying to do enough good to cancel out our bad. And as we saw in the last lesson, that's a *lot* of bad! But God set a perfect standard that we cannot live up to, even if we work at it our entire lives. It's impossible for a sinner to reach God's standard of living perfectly every day.

Like Romans 3:10–12 says, "As it is written, There is none righteous, no, not one: There is none that understandeth, there is none that seeketh after God. They are all gone out of the way, they are together become unprofitable; there is none that doeth good, no, not one." Did those verses put enough emphasis on the "not even the nicest person in the world is good enough" to convince you?

This is why salvation is so beautiful. All those hopeless and disgusting words we talked about in the first lesson describe us. We truly need rescuing. If we could possibly be good enough to earn salvation, then accepting Christ as our Rescuer would've been optional. If we could have simply walked out of the burning building some other way, then we wouldn't be so grateful to the firefighter.

But God showed His love to us while we were dead, without hope, His enemies, separated from Him, and willful sinners. That is when Christ died for us. Knowing where you came from greatly impacts who you are now.

Who are you in Christ? You . . . are . . . *saved.*

Please meditate on this for a few minutes, and then write out the testimony of your salvation (God's rescue of your helpless soul) below as if you were telling it to someone who has no concept of what it means to be saved. No need to fake emotion here or any time you share your testimony, but if you really meditate on what it means to be saved, there will be a definite sincerity in how you tell your story.

_____

_____

_____

_____

READ ALL ABOUT IT

Read and meditate on these verses again.

Being justified freely by his grace through the redemption that is in Christ Jesus. (Romans 3:24)

In whom we have redemption through his blood, the forgiveness of sins, according to the riches of his grace. (Ephesians 1:7)

What's It Mean?

Keeping salvation in mind, let's move on to _redeemed_. Look up the word _redemption_ in our good friend the concordance, and write the definition below:

redemption (629)

_____

_____

This word carries the idea of being ransomed. I think we mostly associate a ransom with a person who has been kidnapped, and the kidnapper puts a ransom price on the person's head. The villain wants payment from the person's family or friends to buy the kidnapped person back. In the Bible this is more commonly used to speak of buying someone out of slavery. I doubt that, since most of us were born free, we have any concept of what it's like to be a slave.

Here are a few definitions. A slave is (1) a person who is the property of and wholly subject to another; a bond servant, (2) a person entirely under the domination of some influence or person, or (3) a person who is the legal property of another and is forced to obey them.[2]

What's It Mean to You?

Before salvation we were slaves to sin and Satan. We belonged completely to him, and we had to obey him—no matter what. Satan was a cruel master, even if we didn't realize it at the time. He wanted to keep us chained to our sin until we died, after which he would claim our soul forever in hell. But our Redeemer came and paid for us. And how did He do that?

Romans 6:23 reveals the ransom price that was put on our head: "For the wages [payment] of sin is death."

Therefore, all sinners are automatically condemned to die, but there is more. Write out Romans 5:8.

_____

_____

_____

So the only way to pay for sin is by death, . . . and Christ died. He paid the price in full! This is why Christians write so many songs about the blood of Christ. It probably sounds really weird to unbelievers (and, actually, for a long time I thought it was odd too) to dwell so much on someone's blood. We even observe communion, in which we eat bread and drink juice to remember Christ's body and blood. *Redemption* is why it's so precious to us. Christ gave His own body and blood to buy us back from sin. That's quite the ransom price! This is why Christ as our Redeemer should define us.

WRAP IT UP

Some probably well-meaning Christians could use our redemption and salvation to build self-esteem. "You are so worth it. Christ died for you! Look at how valuable you are. Christ chose to save you, you beautiful, worthy, amazing thing, you!" But think back on the whole plan of salvation. It has *everything* to do with God's grace, and *nothing* to do with how *worth it* we are. Christ reached out to us in His love and mercy, not because He couldn't resist the charms of fabulous, irresistible us. If salvation was based on our merit, worth, or good deeds, we'd be tempted to be proud and to find our security in ourselves. Instead of building ourselves up, salvation humbles us and drives us to find our confidence in the only one who could and who did secure salvation for us—Christ.

Read John 10:28–29. What promise does Christ give regarding our salvation in these verses?

_____

_____

Satan can't take you back. Because of Christ, you've been rescued and ransomed for good. Talk about security!

[DEFINING TRUTH:
Your security for salvation is Christ.

How does the study of the truths about your salvation and redemption affect your thinking about your security struggle? (example: increased thankfulness and praise to God for salvation or a more anchored joy in Christ and all He's done, rather than a focus on how people treat you)

_____

_____

Maybe your insecurity comes out through worrying. What does your salvation and redemption tell you about God that can help you kick your sinful pattern of worry?

_____

_____

We're often afraid to witness to or take a stand around unsaved people because we're afraid of how they'll respond or what they'll think of us. How can these truths affect your boldness when witnessing to unsaved friends?

_____

_____

PUT OFF

1. Confess it and get rid of it

What are some natural attitudes and responses that should be changed by meditating on your salvation and redemption?

_____

_____

Which of those attitudes or responses have been part of your life?

_____

2. Deal with it

Is there someone from whom you need to seek forgiveness (besides God) concerning these attitudes or actions?

_____

3. Cut it out

What is there in your life that you need to amputate to make it harder for you to sin in these areas?

_____

_____

RENEW YOUR MIND

1. Memorize it

Write out the verse that you plan to memorize.

_____

_____

2. Meditate on it

How will this passage keep you focused on your salvation and redemption?

_____

_____

PUT ON

1. Swap it

What actions should you put on as a natural response to your salvation and redemption?

_____

_____

2. Check up on it

Who can you ask to help keep you accountable for the decisions you made this week? When will you talk to this person about helping you?

_____

_____

Some of these changes might be tough to identify, but you can ask someone to catch you when you complain or keep you accountable about your boldness in witnessing or whatever the Lord convicted you about. Biblical accountability is always a good thing!

3 Alive and Justified

et's start with *alive*. You're alive . . . and dead. Huh? For this chapter we're going to refer back to some of the verses in the last lesson. You can either turn to these passages in your Bible or look back at the beginning of the last lesson to reread them.

READ ALL ABOUT IT

Read Romans 6:11, Ephesians 2:1, 4–5, and Colossians 2:13–14, and write down what we are dead to and what we are alive to.

_____

_____

_____

_____

What's It Mean?

I'm not going to make you look up the Greek words for *alive* and *dead*. I'll give you the definitions right now. Get ready. OK. *Alive* means *alive* and *dead* means *dead* or *not alive*. I know, impressive, right? Really, that's about all you'll find if you research them.

Picture This

I saw one of those *Candid Camera*-type shows, where a casket (containing a person *pretending* to be dead) was wheeled into an elevator with one poor, unsuspecting victim at a time. The hidden camera followed the reactions of the person being pranked as he or she tried to stay as far away from the casket as possible, looking nervously around the elevator, obviously anxious to get off. Just as they're about to reach their floor, the top half of the casket door springs open and the *dead* guy flops out. Sometimes he would just hang there, and other times he would turn and smile at them. Needless to say, some pretty hilarious reactions were caught on camera.

We're naturally a little squeamish around dead people, and we certainly don't expect a dead person to move or respond. It just doesn't happen. *Dead* means lifeless. A lifeless person can't do . . . anything!

What's It Mean to You?

Before salvation you were dead to God. Even the good you did couldn't please Him because it was done with no thought about Him. You had no relationship with Him. You were dead, like a cold, stiff spiritual corpse. Flattering, huh?

At salvation we became alive to Him—active, responding to, having a relationship with, and living for Him! At salvation we died to sin. We'll talk a lot more about what that actually means in our next lesson. You're always alive and dead at the same time: first you were alive to sin and dead to God; now you're alive to God and dead to sin. Stay tuned.

READ ALL ABOUT IT

I've got to tell you, I love this next word. I worked at an attorney's office for almost three years and learned quite a few crazy legal terms that helped the word *justification* make so much more sense to me.
Read Romans 3:24 and 5:1, 9.

What's It Mean?

Look up *justified* in your concordance.
justified (1344)

_____

_____

So we're justified . . . whatever that means, right? Don't be intimidated by words like this. It's not actually hard to understand; it's only hard to comprehend *why* God chose to do such an incredible thing for us.

Step one of understanding justification: We are guilty of sinning. I don't think any of us would deny that at this point. There's overwhelming evidence against us, proving that we are guilty.

Step two: Christ was innocent and righteous. You can study Isaiah 53 on your own if you want to see all the times this passage stresses Christ's innocence. Christ was not guilty of committing any sin whatsoever, even though Hebrews 4:15 tells us that He was fully human and was tempted to sin.

Step three: Christ took our sin and guilt. Christ became guilty in our place so that all of God's anger would be poured out on Him instead of on us. This is called *substitutionary atonement*. Don't get intimidated by the big words. That just means that Christ stood in for us, like a substitute teacher does when the real teacher is out.

We're the real culprits; we should've been the ones dying and receiving all of God's wrath for our sin, but instead Christ took the punishment for us. When Christ died, God couldn't even look at His own Son because all our sin and guilt was placed on Him. Even though Jesus never personally sinned, He chose to take all of our sins on Himself. (See Isaiah 53:4–6.) Second Corinthians 5:21 begins, "For he [God] hath made him [Christ] to be sin for us, who knew no sin." So God viewed Christ as guilty, as if He actually committed all of our sins, and God treated Christ like He was the sinner, instead of us.

Step four: We *are* righteous and innocent! Here's the rest of 2 Corinthians 5:21: ". . . that we might be made the righteousness of God in him [Christ]." In the same way Christ took our sin and guilt, He gives us His righteousness. The same way God treated Christ as guilty when He wasn't, God looks at us as righteous when we aren't. Now that payment has been made for sin, everyone who accepts God's free gift of salvation is cleared from all the penalties involved with sin, and we will never experience God's wrath for our sin. Christ experienced that for us. Since sin has been paid for once and for all, God will never look at any believer as personally guilty—ever. Christ won righteous status for all of us. You *are* guilty, but in Christ, you are forever righteous! (Please appreciate how much restraint it is taking on my part, not to fill an entire page with exclamation marks to show how crazy exciting this is!)

Picture This

Think about a courtroom with God as the perfect judge and you as the guilty criminal He just declared innocent of all the crimes you were *seen* committing.

That wouldn't go over very well in our justice system. In fact, every time there has been a case where the jury or judge has let someone off the hook when the public believes them to be guilty, the people are angered.

Even if you were too young to remember the O. J. Simpson trial, I'm sure you've heard about it. It became famous for a verdict that people believed to be completely unjust. More recently, the Casey Anthony trial joined the ranks of unpopular trial outcomes. Casey was a young single mother, whose two-year-old daughter, Caylee, disappeared in 2008. Casey did not report her daughter's disappearance for thirty days and was seen partying during that time, which doesn't exactly make her look like a grieving mother. After it was confirmed that Caylee had been murdered, much evidence was brought against Casey.

It seemed the whole country believed that Casey was guilty of killing her daughter, yet after several years in jail, a jury trial, and the work of a skilled lawyer, Casey was declared not guilty. Social media exploded with normal people and celebrities alike crying for justice for Caylee. Of course, nobody knows who committed the crime. Maybe Casey really did do it; maybe she didn't. Either way, the reaction from America was loud and clear: they were upset that Casey was set free, and as I write this book, no one has yet been punished for the heinous crime committed against a beautiful little girl.

What's It Mean to You?

When we stand in God's courtroom, we *are* guilty. Plain and simple. God's law demands we live a perfect, righteous life with not a single sin in it, and we are incapable of doing that. He has enough evidence against us in one day, not to mention our whole life, to condemn us to death and hell. Yet our perfect judge sent His own Son to take our punishment. Christ, the only one who never broke even one little part of God's law, took our death penalty. Now when God looks at us, He doesn't see our guilt; He sees Christ's righteousness. That doesn't make sense. I can't fathom how God can know all that I've done but look at me and see only the righteousness of His Son.

I love the way John MacArthur explains it in his commentary on Ephesians.

> God knows how we were, how we now live, and how we will live the rest of our lives. He sees everything about us in stark-naked reality. Yet He says, "I am satisfied with you because I am satisfied with My Son, to whom you belong. When I look at you, I see Him, and I am pleased."[1]

Who am I? I am justified!
Read Romans 5:18–19.

The word *condemned* is the opposite of *justified*. *Justified* is the verdict that declares you not guilty. *Condemned* is the verdict that declares that you *are* guilty and earns you the death penalty.

Who was the one man who disobeyed and condemned us all?

_____

What was the one trespass or sin?

_____

What was the one act of righteousness and who completed it to justify us?

_____

Read Romans 8:33–34.

God the righteous judge, who made the law, and His Son, who fulfilled the law's requirements, are the only ones who could condemn you. But they say, "Not Guilty." It's like a big "Case Dismissed" is stamped over your whole life. Check out how God sees you . . . because of Christ.

"He sees you as a person who

- always does the things that are pleasing to him;
- is so focused on accomplishing his will and work that doing so is your daily food;
- doesn't seek your own will but seeks his will instead;
- doesn't seek to receive glory (praise, respect, worship) from others;
- has always kept all his commandments;
- lives in such a way that your life brings holiness to others;
- loves others and lays down your life on a consistent basis;
- lives in such a way that the people around you know that you love your heavenly Father more than anything else;
- seeks to obey every command so that righteousness will be fulfilled."[2]

Wait a minute. Are you thinking with confusion back to the first lesson where we saw that none of that list describes us? Good! You should be. Because only when we truly look at ourselves and then truly look at Christ can we understand the awesomeness of justification. You already have this righteous status forever. Your record is clean right now, tomorrow, and for all of eternity.

No matter how many times you fail God and sin, He still looks at you as righteous because of Christ. Excited yet? Can you see how this completely defines who you are? It's a little hard to focus on what other people think of you and be moody or proud or ungrateful when you know that the God of the universe says you're completely righteous.

Whew. My mind is officially blown. This is all going to come into play in a major way in our next chapter on sin and guilt.

WRAP IT UP

Before you go on to the Put Off, Renew, Put On section, let's get our minds going in the right direction to apply these truths. I realize this study might be a little different from what some of you were expecting. You might be asking, "Why are we doing all this doctrinal stuff? What's this got to do with me defining who I am?"

May I humbly suggest, "Everything!"

We're establishing the difference between how the world tells us to handle our insecurities and how God tells us to. All the verses we've looked at in the last two chapters don't just give you a weak assurance that you're beautiful the way you are, that you're enough, that you're a good person, or that you're worth it. In fact, everything in God's Word tells us just the opposite. My heart is not beautiful. I am not worthy of God's love. My works are not good enough. I am not good.

But Christ is everything that I'm not!

The Bible gives us all we need to know about who we are as Christian young women. Everything we are or can ever hope to be is found in Christ and the riches we have in Him. This knowledge is what guides us when we're with a group of friends, family, strangers, or all alone.

So how do we apply these truths to our thinking and actions? For me as an insecure Pleaser, truths about what God has done for me have totally flipped my priorities. When I look at all the blessings God has given me by saving me, ransoming me, making me alive, and viewing me as righteous, it becomes very insignificant whether or not a person thinks I'm funny, pretty, or popular.

True joy is found in Christ, not in whether you're part of the cool crowd or have boys falling at your feet or have more friends on a social network than somebody else. We can have confidence in who we are, not because of us, but because of Christ. Instead of constantly trying to figure out who we are, we have a Book that spells it out for us. What if a group of people won't include you? You're still justified. What if someone else is the center of attention? You're still saved. What if someone embarrasses you in front of your friends? God ransomed you from Satan! These are the truly important things about you.

Disclaimer: This doesn't mean we should have a *Forget you!* attitude toward people. Knowing who we are in Christ should never puff us up and make us act superior to others. In light of our relationship with God, loving and serving people should be our number one priority. Notice I said *loving* and *serving* people, not *pleasing* people. We have to realize that our goal is to glorify the God who saved us, redeemed us, made us alive, and justified us. We can't focus on that goal if all we care about is looking good in front of our friends or getting a guy to notice us. Plus, it's a little hard to mope about the way someone treats us when our focus is on this amazing God and bringing glory to Him!

Let these truths transform your perspective. First, we have to meditate on all that Christ has done for us and to allow that to flood our lives with gratitude for His amazing grace. Second, we focus on serving people, which also brings Him glory. There's nothing in that list about being popular or well liked. That's not even on the radar.

Now see if you can apply some of these truths to your own insecurity struggles.

DEFINING TRUTH:
Your security for spiritual life and righteousness is Christ.

Here's a silly, personal example to give you a point of reference for one way this study helped me. I'm not very good at sports, and my husband and I work with teens. We play lots of games that give me a chance to look very incompetent in front of the teens. I used to shy away from participating so I wouldn't look stupid. I also used to withdraw from talking to new people, afraid I'd say something dumb.

Studying the last two chapters has helped me realize that the truths found in them are the truly important things about me and not how well I do at sports or how vibrant my personality is. Now I play all the games, and sometimes I even do better at them than I used to because I'm not as concerned about how stupid I look playing them. Who cares if I stink at a game? God looks at me as righteous because of Christ! I know it's a trivial example, but these truths really do apply to the way I deal with my insecurities.

Now think about your life. The Put Off, Renew, Put On section may be harder to define for this lesson, but examine your heart and see if the Lord has convicted you about ways you've been handling your insecurities that are inconsistent with how He wants you to handle them.

PUT OFF

1. Confess it and get rid of it

What specific sinful patterns in your thinking or actions has the Holy Spirit revealed to you?

_____

_____

2. Deal with it

Have your wrong views affected the way you deal with people? Who is there (besides God) that you need to ask for forgiveness?

_____

_____

3. Cut it out

What sinful thoughts and actions do you need to remove from your life so that your security is grounded in Christ?

_____

_____

Renew Your Mind

1. Memorize it

Write out the verse that you plan to memorize.

_____

_____

2. Meditate on it

How will this passage help you focus on your security in Christ?

\
\

PUT ON

1. Swap it

What thoughts or actions do you need to make your priority?

\
\

2. Check up on it

Who can you ask to keep you accountable? (Note: You don't have to find a different person for each struggle.) When will you talk to this person about helping you?

\
\

4 Dead to Sin

n this first section of our study, we've been looking at sin. Sin is what drives us to see our need for a Savior. Sin is what brought about the need for Christ to die. If we accept God's salvation, we're saved, redeemed, and justified.

So, that's it. No more sin! Fabulous. Wouldn't that be nice?

Unfortunately, sin still exists in the world and in every individual Christian. In this chapter we're going to look at our relationship with sin now that we're saved, and what our relationship with sin *should* be because of Christ.

READ ALL ABOUT IT

Turn to Romans 6, and read verses 1–14 (I'm not writing all those out, so you have to actually turn there this time. Off you go.)

That's always been a confusing passage for me. To summarize the main point of those verses, let's try to break it down into manageable pieces. Be sure to reread the verses as I mention them because, unless you're Super Memory Girl, you probably won't remember what the verses were talking about.

What's It Mean?

In verses 1 and 2, Paul is addressing a big concern about the doctrine of justification. That sounds scary, but it's not; you know what it means now. Review: What is justification?

_____

_____

God says that we're dressed in Christ's righteousness and that will never change, no matter what. So some people think that means that I am free to sin as much as I want since God will still see Christ's righteousness when He looks at sinful me. I love Paul's response. Sometimes old English is hard to understand, but not here. He basically says, "Are you crazy? No way! You're dead to sin, so how can you act like you're alive to it?" Paul couldn't imagine anyone using justification as an excuse for sin.

I don't know about you, but just reading the list on page 32 about my record before God makes me want to live up to that record (even though I never perfectly can here on earth). Christ gave me this perfect record when I accepted His salvation. If I say, "Yeah, well, God says I'm righteous no matter what, so now I can live however I want," I show that I truly don't understand salvation and justification.

Romans 6:3–5 tells us that we're united (or one) with Christ now, since we put our faith in Him and His work on the cross. His death, burial, and resurrection became our death, burial, and resurrection, because we're identified with Him. So anytime this passage says something about Christ, you can include yourself with Him. Christ died, so we died; Christ was raised, so we're raised.

I love verses 6 and 7. What does verse 6 tell us happened to our old self?

_____

_____

Our old nature is dead, and now we have a new nature. However, until we get to heaven, we still have our fallen human body, which the Bible sometimes calls our flesh. Specifically, our minds and thoughts are still infected by our sin nature and will tempt us to do things that don't fit in with our new nature. Don't get confused, because this is where it falls into place. Depending on what version of the Bible you're using, verse 6 says your body of sin (your old nature and sinful desires) is *destroyed* or *brought to nothing*. That means your old nature is made completely powerless.

Romans 6:7 is talking about Christians when it says, "For he that is dead." (So this is talking about you. You died because you're identified with Christ, and He died.) The rest of the verse says that the one who died (that's you) "is freed from sin." The Greek word for *freed* is the same Greek word as *justified*. Unless you're a Greek geek, you're probably saying, "So what?"

Here's the *so what*. Paul is strengthening his argument. People were thinking, "I'm allowed to sin all I want because I'm justified." Paul is saying you don't have to sin anymore *because you're justified*. You're free! Because of Christ, God declared you righteous, and now your old sinful desires have lost their power over you. You don't have to give in.

What's It Mean to You?

Have you ever felt sin's pull so strongly that you were absolutely sure you couldn't resist it? Maybe some friends were telling a juicy story, you had some extra details, and you just *had* to participate in the gossip. Maybe it was that time of the month, and you felt like you *had* to bite someone's head off because you just couldn't help it. Maybe you were just so tired that you *had* to sleep in instead of reading your Bible.

Write down one time in the last week that you felt like you just *had* to sin, and you gave in to that desire.

_____

_____

We've all felt like this at one time or other, but what is amazing about Romans 6 is that according to God (who never gets it wrong) *we don't have to give into sin!* Girls, this can be life changing. When we realize who we are in Christ, our entire relationship to sin can change.

Picture This

One particular day I just did not feel like having my devotions. At the time, my husband and I were struggling through a trial in our lives, and the last thing I wanted to do was to read my Bible. I had time for it during the day, but I did everything else I could think to do. I had time for it that evening, but I chose to spend my time watching the Food Network instead.

I was halfway through my cooking show when it suddenly hit me: *I don't have to do this!* I actually sat upright on the couch with the realization. In fact, I don't even remember a time in my life when this was so clear: *I'm free from the power of sin. The desire I have to lie around and do nothing and ignore my time with the Lord is a sin. So I'm free from it. I don't have to obey this desire!*

I considered waiting until the show was over, but these verses came barreling through my mind again. I shut the TV off and got out my Bible. My time with the Lord that night was some of the best, most encouraging time I'd had in weeks. And the rest of the night, I was pretty excited that the Lord had helped me resist temptation. Obviously, this isn't a major victory, but I'll take it.

What's It Mean to You?

Romans 6:8–10 tells us that Christ died to sin, that we died with Christ, and that we now *live unto God*. What do you think it means to *live unto God*?

_____

_____

Verse 11 brings the point home, so follow Paul's reasoning. Christ died to sin, meaning He paid the penalty for sin, and He broke the power of sin over us. We are in Christ or identified with Him. Therefore, *we* died to sin. He uses the words *reckon* or *consider*, which are words expressing confidence in a fact. He wants us to accept by faith that, because of Christ, sin has no power over us.

Sometimes it's hard to accept that, isn't it? Often we're so used to giving in to the demands of our sinful desires that it just seems like we can't resist, even if we want to. I've felt like that many times. It's at those times that we have to confidently accept by faith that this is a fact: I'm dead to sin and alive to God.

[DEFINING TRUTH:
Because of Christ, I don't have to live a defeated Christian life.

I love the awesome word pictures in Romans 6:12 and 14: "Let not sin therefore reign in your mortal body, that ye should obey it in the lusts thereof. . . . For sin shall not have dominion over you: for ye are not under the law, but under grace."

What job description comes to mind when you hear the words *reign* and *dominion*?

_____

Picture This

A king rules over a kingdom and dictates what goes on in that kingdom. If his country is invaded and he's overthrown and cast into prison, he is no longer able to reign over his kingdom. Before we were saved, our sin nature was our king, and we obeyed every little desire our sinful flesh presented. When Jesus came and ransomed us from Satan, Jesus destroyed the king of our heart (sin), and Christ became our King. Sin (my old, sinful desires) may still be lurking in the dungeon of my life, but King Sin has absolutely no power over me anymore. He can't give me orders from the dungeon! He has no right to dictate what I do because he is no longer my master and king.

Guess what else verse 12 reveals? It tells us that we can still *allow* sin to control us. Even though the power of sin to control us is completely defeated, we can still creep down to the dungeon and take orders from this defeated king. Verse 12 is a command. It says, "Don't let sin control you!" It's a choice. Our sinful desires are called our *passions* or *lusts*. These desires are "a longing, especially for what is forbidden." It seems ridiculous that we still gravitate toward taking orders from that crippled, defeated, broken, powerless king of sin when our powerful, glorious, loving, reigning King is alive and telling us not to give in to the longings that He forbids. We don't have to, but we so often do.

Is there a sin (maybe more than one) in your life that you're continually struggling with and that you just keep going back to? What is it?

_____

_____

Even as Christians, we can see that sin and temptation are still very active in our lives. So when the Bible says that we are "dead to sin," it's a little hard to believe. It sure doesn't feel like I'm dead to it. This doesn't mean that when we get saved, sin is completely dead, and we don't have to worry about it anymore. It means that Christ crushed the *power* of sin over us, and even though it's a constant fight like Paul acknowledges in Romans 7:15–24, we already know that we're the winners. We just have to live—through faith in God's promise—like sin has no power over us.

Do you see how this relates to your relationship with sin? Pretty incredible, right? It shouldn't be a very exciting fight for Satan to be involved in since his power over Christians is defeated, but we make it more interesting for him by choosing to obey our sinful lusts. Christ has already won the battle over sin, death, and hell, and we just have to claim His victory. Look up Romans 8:37, and write the three words it uses to describe a Christian because of Christ:

_____

_____

In the Greek, this phrase means *over-conquerors*. It means "to conquer so completely that there isn't even a threat to your personal life or health."[1] That's the kind of victory in a battle I can get behind!

Because of who you are in Christ, you're an over-conqueror! When you feel at your very weakest spiritually, *you can claim His victory.* When you think you're so deeply involved in your sin that you can never get out, *you can claim His victory.* When you're enjoying your sin so much that you just can't imagine your life without it, *you can claim His victory.* When you've tried so many times to defeat the same sin and have failed the same number of times, *you can claim His victory.* The possibilities are endless!

We can also know that this fight against sin will not go on forever. Look at Romans 7:24–25: "O wretched man that I am! who shall deliver me from the body of this death? I thank God through Jesus Christ our Lord. So then with the mind I myself serve the law of God. . . ." Paul is ready to throw his hands up in despair over this constant battle with his sin nature. Who will deliver him from this fight someday?

What event(s) marks the end of a Christian's fight?

Whew, this is life-changing stuff. If we could perfectly grasp this, we'd have a lot of super Christians walking around. But each day, we just have to take steps by faith to deny our sinful desires at every turn. It's a growth process, and it's a battle. It's called *sanctification*. And it's possible—because of Christ!

Picture This

This is a tale of two coupons. Michael took me to an outlet mall last weekend (because he's the best husband ever). We brought two coupons with us for two of our favorite stores. At the first store, we weren't even close to spending enough to use the coupon. There was a girl in front of me in the checkout line who had been very rude to me all throughout the store. Every time I turned around she was pushing past me to get to the rack I was looking at, and it seemed like she was purposefully boxing me out. It was pretty annoying. I overheard her in the checkout line complaining to her friend that she was spending a lot of money . . . enough money to use my coupon. I went through a little heart tug of war. I didn't want to give the rude girl my coupon for 15 percent off, but the coupon was going to just rot in my purse since I couldn't use it, and it seemed like a prime opportunity to show biblical love to an unlovely person. So I tapped her on the shoulder and offered it to her. Man, did her attitude toward me change! I knew I had done what Jesus would've wanted me to do even if I didn't feel like it. Victory!

On to coupon two: Next we shopped at my husband's favorite store, and he bought several shirts for work, and then we left the outlets. We were on a weekend trip, and on our way back home the next day, Michael decided to return to the same store to buy a suit that was on sale. His purchase was just ten dollars short of the total needed to use our great coupon. I was in a horrid mood. I was worn out, did not feel like shopping, and did not feel like spending more money. I was determined to save money, so even though Michael informed me that what I wanted to do was tacky, I went to the front and asked the cashier if we could go to the car and get the shirts we'd bought yesterday, return them, and ring them up again so we could get the discount. She hem-hawed around and said that she'd do it but that she wasn't supposed to.

That should've been my answer. But instead of saying I'd never dream of making her do something against the rules, I said, "All right then, I'll go get the shirts." And I was rather snippy about it too. Go ahead; gasp at me; I deserve it. Thankfully, Michael was in a more spiritual frame of mind and said firmly that if she wasn't supposed to, we wouldn't ask her to. He bought another shirt, and we used the coupon I was so obsessed with. It took me a while, but I finally realized that I had given a horrible impression of Christ to that cashier—not that she knew I was a Christian. But based on our interaction, she would never have guessed that I was. And that was the problem. By giving in to my sinful, rotten attitude, I missed an opportunity to show Christ in my life.

WRAP IT UP

What was the point of those two long stories? They happened within twenty-four hours of each other. In one situation, I fought the power of sin in my life and glorified Christ, even if they didn't know I was a Christian. In the other situation, I gave in to my fleshly desires and made someone's life harder, not better. You and I can't get complacent. We have to fight sin and claim Christ's victory over the power of sin in our lives on a daily, moment-by-moment basis, so that we can take every opportunity to show Christ to others around us.

[**DEFINING TRUTH:**
In Christ I have victory over sin.

PUT OFF

1. Confess it and get rid of it

In what specific sin struggles in your life are you refusing to claim Christ's victory?

_____

_____

2. Deal with it

How does your lack of victory over sin affect other people? Who do you need to ask for forgiveness?

_____

_____

3. Cut it out

What do you need to cut out of your life to make it harder for you to keep going back to your sin? How will you do that?

_____

_____

Renew Your Mind

1. Memorize it

Write out the verse that you plan to memorize.

_____

_____

_____

2. Meditate on it

How will this passage help you gain victory over sin?

_____

_____

PUT ON

1. Swap it

With what biblical thoughts and actions do you need to replace your sinful ones?

_____

_____

What is your plan to start incorporating these thoughts and actions into your life?

_____

2. Check up on it

Who are you going to ask to keep you accountable as you seek to conquer your sin struggles? When are you going to talk to them about helping you?

_____

_____

5 Free from Guilt

et's look at guilt, shall we? To me *guilt* is one of those words that sound like what they mean, but maybe that's just because I *know* what it means. It sounds like a heavy word, a word that is not very nice; kind of like a combination of *guillotine* and *gluttony—guilty*.

READ ALL ABOUT IT

Read the following two verses, substituting the word *guilt* whenever you see the word *iniquity* or *iniquities*.

For thy name's sake, O Lord, pardon mine iniquity [guilt]; for it is great. (Psalm 25:11)

And I will cleanse them from all their iniquity [guilt], whereby they have sinned against me; and I will pardon all their iniquities [guilt], whereby they have sinned, and whereby they have transgressed against me. (Jeremiah 33:8)

What's It Mean?

The dictionary defines *guilt* in two ways: (1) the fact or state of having committed an offense, crime, violation, or wrong, especially against moral or penal law, or (2) a feeling of responsibility or remorse for some offense, crime, wrong, etc., whether real or imagined.[1]

Both definitions work in a Christian sense, as well a secular one. Before you were saved, did the first definition of guilt apply to you?

_____

Does it apply to you now that you're a Christian?

_____

Why or why not?

_____

_____

We are all sinners, and we are all guilty of breaking God's law. At salvation God gave us Christ's righteousness. Now instead of being guilty, Christians are described by Romans 4:7–8: "Blessed are they whose iniquities are forgiven, and whose sins are covered. Blessed is the man to whom the Lord will not impute sin."

You were enjoying the break from Greek, weren't you? Break's over! Look up the following words from those verses.

blessed (3107)

_____

_____

forgiven (863)

_____

_____

covered (1943)

_____

_____

impute or count (3049)

_____

_____

Now, use the definitions you found to rephrase Romans 4:7–8 in your own words.

_____

_____

_____

Picture This

Let's explore the word *impute* or *count*. It's just too cool not to.

My parents work at a Christian camp, and my mom runs the craft shop there. Campers can paint plaster or wood, stamp leather projects, or make beaded necklaces and earrings. Several times a year, she has to take inventory of everything in the store and report it to the financial officers of the camp. Inventory means counting. Everything. Even little tiny beads. Yeah, it's a big job.

We used to have inventory parties and invite lots of friends to stay late into the night, eating junk food while counting every item in the store. You could hear the murmurs of people trying not to lose their place while counting hundreds of individual and packaged beads and adding them up on paper or counting on fingers, trying to get the most accurate number possible. Often we would discover more of a certain color bead hiding with a different section, and we would have to go re-figure our final tally. I'm sure we never quite got a perfect count.

What's It Mean to You?

But the Lord is omniscient, meaning that He knows everything and can't forget anything. He is aware of every sin I've ever committed or ever will commit. And He promised me that He will not take inventory of my sin! He isn't in heaven counting how many times, just today, my attitude stunk or I chose not to do the right thing. He doesn't have a piece of paper titled "Natalie's Sins" to which He is continually adding angry, accusing words. Like we saw earlier, this doesn't give me permission to say, "Hurray! Now I get to go live however I want; say whatever I want; do whatever I want!"

Look up 1 Corinthians 1:8, and from this verse tell who will sustain you so that you will be guiltless (or unable to be accused) when you get to heaven. You may need to glance back at verses 4–7 to get the context.

_____

_____

Always remember that your guiltless status has nothing to do with you and everything to do with who you are in Christ. God's amazing grace actually makes me want to please Him more because His grace sees me as not guilty of breaking His law. In God's eyes, this legal definition of *guilt* no longer applies to me: the fact or state of having committed an offense, crime, violation, or wrong, especially against moral or penal law.

However, read Romans 14:12. Let's take a teeny, tiny rabbit trail. Let's turn Greek geek one more time. Even though the Lord doesn't count my sins, I will still be accountable to Him when I get to heaven. I will have to report to Him, whether or not I lived my life on earth to bring Him glory. There's a connection with the word *impute*, or *count*, and the word *account* in Romans 14:12. I'm not a Greek expert by *any* stretch of the imagination, but *count* comes from the root word for *account*, which means *something said or thought*.

Even though God won't take inventory of our sins, and we won't ever have to suffer the penalty for our sins, someday in heaven we are still going to have to lay out everything we've ever thought or done before Him, and we will be rewarded accordingly. So there's another motivation for us to live like we're dead to sin: we will be accountable to God for our life. (Sorry, I just thought the connection was too good to ignore.)

On to definition number two, which deals with a *feeling* of guilt, whether legitimate or not. One kind of guilt can actually be godly sorrow over your sin that comes from the Holy Spirit. We call this conviction. This is when we realize that we've sinned and need to take care of it with the Lord. Obviously, this is legitimate guilt, and one of the blessings of being a child of God is that He won't let us continue in our sin without pointing it out to us.

Another kind of guilt is sinful. It could come when we reject the promises of forgiveness that God has clearly given us and choose to focus on a feeling that comes from what others say or from what we decide to believe. Or we might put a standard of performance on ourselves, like thinking we have to do certain things to be accepted in God's eyes—things that God never commands us to do.

READ ALL ABOUT IT

Compare the two sections below and identify which is godly sorrow over sin and which focuses on a feeling of guilt caused by unwillingness to believe that God can and will forgive.

> O Lord, rebuke me not in thy wrath: neither chasten me in thy hot displeasure. For thine arrows stick fast in me, and thy hand presseth me sore. There is no soundness in my flesh because of thine anger; neither is there any rest in my bones because of my sin. For mine iniquities are gone over mine

head: as an heavy burden they are too heavy for me. My wounds stink and are corrupt because of my foolishness. I am troubled; I am bowed down greatly; I go mourning all the day long. For my loins are filled with a loathsome disease: and there is no soundness in my flesh. I am feeble and sore broken: I have roared by reason of the disquietness of my heart. Lord, all my desire is before thee; and my groaning is not hid from thee. My heart panteth, my strength faileth me: as for the light of mine eyes, it also is gone from me. . . . My lovers and my friends stand aloof from my sore; and my kinsmen stand afar off. For I am ready to halt, and my sorrow is continually before me. For I will declare mine iniquity; I will be sorry for my sin. (Psalm 38:1–11, 17–18)

Do you think this Psalm demonstrates someone who is experiencing a feeling of sinful guilt or conviction from God?

_____

What words in the Psalm make you think that?

_____

_____

Now, read the testimony of Milton Vincent, the author of *A Gospel Primer for Christians*:

> I would never have acknowledged this to be the case at the time, but I labored for most of my life to maintain my justified status before God, and I was always left frustrated in my attempts to do so. The "God" I believed in was frequently angered at me. When I would come into His presence to make right some wrong, His arms were tightly folded, and His eyes were slow to meet mine. I imagined an angry look on His face, and it was always up to me to figure out some way to mollify Him. I figured that if I beat myself up sufficiently in His presence, or pled with Him long enough, or just waited a few hours to put a little distance between me and my sin, then He might warm to me again. Driving home from work one day, my mind came back to the Lord after I had allowed my thoughts to drift for about

ten minutes. My mind began to agitate and I winced under the Lord's gaze. "Lord, are we OK?'" I asked. "Have I thought any thoughts that have offended You? Do I need to make anything right in order to restore our relationship?" A feeling of nausea began to sweep over me, and years of pent-up frustration seemed to coalesce in that one moment. "Surely, relating to God can't be this difficult," my heart screamed. "Why is it so hard to stay in His good graces? I can't keep track of every thought in order to make sure that He stays favorably disposed to me! That isn't possible!"[1]

Does this sound like someone who is experiencing sinful guilt or conviction from God?

_____

What makes you think that?

_____

_____

Have you ever felt like Milton Vincent did after you've sinned? Have you ever had a hard time believing that God actually forgave you after you confessed a sin to Him or that you had to do something to make Him like you again? What was the situation and when did you finally feel like everything was back to normal between you and God?

_____

_____

_____

In Mr. Vincent's defense, that was his testimony of what spurred him on to write an amazing book about the gospel, salvation, and justification. (He figured out that he didn't have to live in that guilt, in case you were mentally beating him up about it.)

Sinful guilt surfaces when we choose not to believe that God mercifully rescued us from sin and declared us righteous because of Christ. Maybe you have what people might label as *major sins* in your past, and you just can't believe that God wiped your slate clean when you accepted His salvation. Maybe you struggle with guilt every time you commit any sin, and you confess it over and over again, hoping that one of those times, God will actually believe you're sorry and forgive you. Maybe you've set up a standard of spirituality for yourself, and you feel guilty if you don't reach it. Talk about living a life of insecurity!

Read Romans 8:1 and 33. Rephrase these two verses in your own words.

Sometimes you don't or won't *feel* forgiven. If you struggle with sinful guilt, you have to claim these two verses and realize that they're true because God said so. It doesn't matter how you feel. If you've truly confessed your sin to God, He has forgiven you and won't hold it against you. Simple as that.

I love this quote from John MacArthur: "Forgiveness in Jesus Christ is undeserved, but it is free and it is complete. Those who have Him have freedom from sin, now and throughout eternity. In Christ our sins—past, present, and future—'are forgiven . . . for His name's sake.' (1 John 2:12; cf. Eph. 4:32; Col. 2:13). They were forgiven countless ages before we committed them and will remain forgiven forever."[2]

What a huge promise from our Lord who never lies!

Read Psalm 51 and then Psalm 32. Don't worry; they're not that long. As you read, look for the contrasts David presents of before and after he confessed his sin.

David truly expresses confidence in the Lord's forgiveness. He obviously experienced the crushing weight of conviction of his sin first, but after he confesses it, he wholeheartedly claims the Lord's forgiveness.

Which of David's sins is the topic of these Psalms? (The heading of Psalm 51 may tell you, or you can look at 2 Samuel 12.)

I think we would all tend to classify David's sin as major. Chances are most of us don't know a lot of people who have committed both adultery and murder. Yet I love how David opens Psalm 32 in verses one and two: "Blessed is he whose transgression is forgiven, whose sin is covered. Blessed is the man unto whom the Lord imputeth not iniquity, and in whose spirit there is no guile."

You already know from earlier in this lesson that *blessed* means "How happy!" Even though that was a Greek word and this is Hebrew, they mean the same thing. *Happy* certainly seems like the opposite of *guilty* to me. David recounts how his body and spirit reacted when he was living in sin and then when he was under conviction. He experienced the full depth of the guilt of his sin, but after He asked the Lord's forgiveness, he knew that the guilt was over. Because God loves and promises to forgive, David could say he was happy and blessed.

David's sin was very public too, wasn't it? No doubt, his kingdom knew about it, and probably even his enemies knew about it. He still had to live with the consequences of his sin. His son died, and he was responsible for that. It would have been very easy for David to continue to wallow in the shame of his guilt. His enemies probably threw his failure back in his face whenever they could, yet David knew that he was forgiven and that God viewed him as righteous. He continued to live a successful, passionate life serving the Lord after this major mess-up. He didn't let guilt control him.

We all have a tendency to rank sins, don't we? We think that certain sins are not as bad as others. So if we never murder or are immoral like David, or if we're not addicted to drugs or . . . whatever we think of as a *major* sin, we casually believe that we don't need to be as convicted as David was in those psalms. But that's completely false. *Every* sin put Christ on the cross. *Every* sin validly makes us guilty in God's sight, which is why Christ's act of completely freeing us from guilt defines us. We *should* have to wallow in our helpless guilt forever; but because of Christ, we're free to live happy, blessed lives!

WRAP IT UP

Christ's act of declaring you righteous frees you forever from having to carry around your guilt. He took all your guilt on Himself at the cross and defeated its hold on you. It's not enough to just stop beating yourself up about things in your past. Because again, that'd be something you have to do to fix everything. Just like every other topic we've studied, you can't find the answer in yourself. You have to claim the position that Christ won for you: free from guilt. "How happy" can completely define your life because of who you are in Christ.

To get your mind moving in the right direction for the Put Off, Renew, and Put On sections, answer the questions below.

Has anyone ever tried to make you feel guilty for something that wasn't a sin or for a sin that you'd already confessed and taken care of?

_____

_____

What should your response be in your heart and to them?

_____

_____

When you feel guilt, believing that you're not forgiven for something, how does it affect your attitude and the way you interact with people?

_____

_____

How does it affect your relationship with God?

_____

Are you struggling with sinful guilt over something from your past that you've already confessed, but you just don't feel like God has forgiven you? If so, what issue are you still struggling with?

_____

_____

Do you put unattainable standards on yourself, such as commands that are not in the Bible, to make you feel more spiritual or acceptable to God? What do you require of yourself?

_____

_____

Do you struggle with sinful guilt when you don't reach these goals?

_____

_____

What attitude do you need to confess to the Lord about this sinful guilt?

_____

_____

What promise of God do you need to claim to get rid of that sinful guilt for good and accept your status as forgiven and happy?

_____

[**DEFINING TRUTH:**
Your security for freedom from guilt
is Christ.

PUT OFF

1. Confess it and get rid of it

Is there true guilt or conviction in your heart over a sin that you haven't confessed to the Lord? Identify the sin(s) that you need to confess, and then confess each to the Lord.

_____

_____

2. Deal with it

Has your sinful guilt caused you to sin against any other people? If so, who do you need to ask for forgiveness?

_____

_____

3. Cut it out

What habits are in your life that you need to cut out, to make it harder for you to keep going back to your guilt?

_____

_____

RENEW YOUR MIND

What passages of Scripture or characteristics about God do you need to mediate on?

1. Memorize it

Write out the verse that you plan to memorize.

_____

_____

_____

2. Meditate on it

How will this passage renew your mind?

_____

_____

PUT ON

1. Swap it

What attitudes and actions do you need to put on in place of your sinful guilt feelings?

_____

_____

2. Check up on it

Who can you ask to check up on you to make sure you are not continuing to believe the lie that God can't or won't forgive you? When will you talk to this person about helping you?

_____

_____

SECTION 2
Who Am I in Christ in Relation to God?

6 God's Friend

Friendship is important at any age, but we put a special emphasis on friends during our teen and college years. Whenever my husband asks the teens at our church what topics they'd like to study as a group, without fail, several of them answer with variations on friends, how to be a good friend, or how to make godly friends. It's just naturally at the forefront of their minds.

When I say *friend*, who is the first person that comes to your mind?

_____

What are some characteristics that make this person a good friend to you?

_____

_____

Have you ever thought of God as your friend? I don't think I really did. Maybe that's because the Bible doesn't have a specific verse that says, "You are God's friend." But as I went through this study, I discovered that a big word I'd never really understood before basically just means that I'm God's friend. That word is *reconciliation*.

READ ALL ABOUT IT

*Therefore being justified by faith, we have peace with God through our Lord Jesus Christ: . . . For if, when we were enemies, we were **reconciled** to God by the death of his Son, much more, being **reconciled**, we shall be saved by his life. And not only so, but we also joy in God through our Lord Jesus Christ, by whom we have now received the atonement.* (Romans 5:1, 10–11)

What's It Mean?

Verse 10 tells us that we were God's enemies. I won't make you write down the name of your enemy. Honestly, I can't think of a human that is my personal enemy. I can think of some people that I don't like as much or that I don't click with as well as with other people, but an enemy is more than that. It's someone who has declared war against you. An enemy is a rival, an opponent, an adversary (and I'm not just talking about rival sports teams.) In fact, the Greek word for *enemy* comes from the root that means *to hate, hateful,* or *hostile*.

The best example of a true enemy that I can think of is one of the terrorists who attacked the United States on September 11, 2001. He hated everything our country loves and stands for. He delighted in seeing our country in pain. He actively sought ways to destroy us.

This is what Satan is to God. He completely and utterly hates everything that God is, and if Satan had the power, he would destroy God and all those who belong to Him. The Bible says that we were the exact same way before salvation.

If you were saved at an early age, as I was, you probably have a hard time thinking of yourself as ever being an enemy of God. You probably think that the worst thing you ever did was to tell a little lie or act a little selfish. It's hard to remember hating good and delighting in evil. But even if you were only four years old, you were on Satan's side. You were at war with God and hated everything about Him and what He wanted you to do. You lived to please only yourself and not God. You sinned (even if your sins weren't what we usually view as *major* sins) in direct defiance of God's commands. You were God's enemy. That's a pretty strong word!

Three words stand out in Romans 5:1, 10, and 11: *peace, reconciled*, and *reconciliation* (or *atonement*). Write the definitions you find in your concordance for these words.

peace (1515)

_____

_____

reconciled (2644)

_____

_____

reconciliation (atonement) (2643)

_____

_____

What's It Mean to You?

Stay with me, because this is incredible. We looked at *justification*, (see how often this idea comes up!) which focuses on our standing with God legally. He gives us Christ's innocent, righteous record because of Christ's payment for our sin. However, *reconciliation* and *peace* are terms of friendship. Not only is our *legal standing* with God different, our *personal relationship* with Him is different. The Greek word for peace comes from a verb that means *to become one again*. We were

God's personal enemies, fighting against Him, but now we have peace because we no longer have to fear God's wrath. We often think of peace as a feeling, but it's actually a position and a reality. The war is ended, and there is peace. We're united with God and on His side.

According to Romans 5:1, who made it possible for us to have peace with God?

_____

According to Colossians 1:20, how did He make peace possible?

_____

Picture This

Can you imagine one of the terrorists responsible for the 9-11 attacks walking right up to the president of the United States, asking forgiveness for killing thousands of Americans, being granted forgiveness without a trial, given a clean and innocent record, and then set free to live in New York? Imagine if, on top of that, the president invited the terrorist over to the White House to drink a Coke with him every once in a while. Basically the president allows the terrorist to become a friend of America.

This just would not happen, no matter how apologetic the terrorist was or how forgiving the American people were. There are harsh consequences to becoming an enemy of the United States.

However, this is what God has done for us on an even larger scale. We were guilty, without a doubt, of sinning and breaking His laws. We waged war against God every day of our lives until we became Christians. At that point, God accepted Christ's sacrifice on our behalf and gave us Christ's perfect record. He legally accepts us as innocent (*justification*). But on top of that, even though we were His active enemies, assaulting everything He is by sinning every day, He embraces us and says, "Now we're joined together. You're my dear friend. Come spend time with me." Just like that.

It's one thing to legally declare someone innocent. It's another thing to make that enemy your friend. Like you saw in the definitions for *reconcile* and *reconciliation*, there has been a complete one-hundred-eighty-degree change, and now we're restored to God's favor. We went from enemy to friend at the very moment of our salvation.

Notice how many times in Romans 5:1, 10, and 11 Paul tied Christ to the reconciliation process: peace **through Christ**, reconciled **by His death**, atonement **through Christ**! It's almost every time these words are mentioned! This is a miraculous change; it is a change that we were totally incapable of bringing about. It's like Christ is our mutual friend who introduced us to God. We couldn't just barge into God's presence and demand to be at peace with Him any more than a guilty terrorist could do that to the president of the United States. We needed Christ to reconcile us to God.

Who am I in Christ? I am God's friend!

What's It Mean to You?

Look back at the characteristics you wrote on page 65 about what makes a good friend, and then read through the following verses about God—your friend—and write down the words you find that describe who He is or what He does. You can substitute words that you'd use to describe your modern-day friend if you're not familiar with the words used in your Bible.

But thou, O Lord, art a God full of compassion, and gracious, longsuffering, and plenteous in mercy and truth. (Psalm 86:15)

My friend is

_____

_____

The Lord is nigh unto all them that call upon him, to all that call upon him in truth. (Psalm 145:18)

My friend is

_____

_____

Trust in him at all times; ye people, pour out your heart before him: God is a refuge for us. Selah. (Psalm 62:8)

My friend is

_____

_____

The Lord is my rock, and my fortress, and my deliverer; my God, my strength, in whom I will trust; my buckler, and the horn of my salvation, and my high tower. (Psalm 18:2)

What does "The Lord is my rock" actually mean? Stable? Strong? Unchanging? Make it personal! My friend is

_____

_____

Behold, God is my salvation; I will trust, and not be afraid: for the Lord Jehovah is my strength and my song; he also is become my salvation. (Isaiah 12:2)

My friend is

_____

_____

My goodness, and my fortress; my high tower, and my deliverer; my shield, and he in whom I trust. . . . (Psalm 144:2)

My friend is

_____

_____

For thou, Lord, art good, and ready to forgive; and plenteous in mercy unto all them that call upon thee. (Psalm 86:5)

My friend is

The Lord hath appeared of old unto me, saying, Yea, I have loved thee with an everlasting love: therefore with loving-kindness have I drawn thee. (Jeremiah 31:3)

My friend is

God is our refuge and strength, a very present help in trouble. (Psalm 46:1)

My friend is

Our help is in the name of the Lord, the maker of heaven and earth. (Psalm 124:8)

My friend is

Thine, O Lord, is the greatness, and the power, and the glory, and the victory, and the majesty: for all that is in the heaven and in the earth is thine; thine is the kingdom, O LORD, and thou art exalted as head above all. Both riches and honour come of thee, and thou reignest over all; and in thine hand is power and might; and in thine hand it is to make great, and to give strength unto all. (1 Chronicles 29:11–12)

My friend is

_____

_____

I am the LORD, and there is none else, there is no God beside me: I girded thee, though thou hast not known me: that they may know from the rising of the sun, and from the west, that there is none beside me. I am the LORD, and there is none else. I form the light, and create darkness: I make peace, and create evil: I the LORD do all these things. (Isaiah 45:5–7)

My friend is

_____

_____

I wanted you to discover two things from that exercise. First, I hope that you were encouraged by what you found out about God. He is unlike any human friend we could ever have. My husband, Michael, is a pretty awesome best friend, but as wonderful as he is and as much as I love him, I can't say half those things about him that I wrote about God. God is truly the best friend we could ever have.

Second, you should be humbled, shocked, and amazed that you can call God your friend! I hope you noticed the progression in the verses from comforting and wonderful truths about God to overwhelming and mind-blowing ones. He created us. He saved us. He made the world. He owns the world. He controls the world. *And because of Christ, He is my Friend.* Wow!

Have you ever had a fight with a friend to the extent that you didn't even think of them as a friend for a while?

After that fight you had to, at some point, make up with them before your fellowship was restored. You know that God is the best friend you could ever have, but friendship is a two-way street. You should have a desire to be God's friend out of thankfulness for His friendship to you. The reconciliation that Christ accomplished for you is like justification in that it happened at salvation, and nothing you do can ever change it. You're no longer God's enemy, but His friend, no matter what. Christ ended the war between you and God the moment you got saved. Yet just as learning that God sees you as righteous should make you want to work to become righteous, knowing that you're joined with God in a friend relationship should make you want to be a good friend.

Only one person in the Bible is called God's friend. Take a guess at who it is.

_____

Now turn to James 2:23 and see if you were right. Who was it?

_____

Turn to each of the passages listed below and record the action or characteristic that earned this man the title "Friend of God."

Genesis 12:1–4

_____

_____

Genesis 18:22–33

_____

_____

Genesis 22:1–19

_____

_____

Romans 4:3, 17–21

_____

_____

Hebrews 11:8–10

_____

_____

Here are a few of the major themes of Abraham's life that you should've picked up on:

- obedience no matter what
- sacrifice no matter how hard
- faith and belief in God's promises no matter how long it took for them to be fulfilled

Those sound like characteristics of a pretty good friend of God to me! Abraham was certainly not perfect in any of those areas. He messed up quite a few times, yet the Bible still calls him God's friend. The common bond between all of those passages is Abraham's communication with God. He always listened to what God commanded, talked to God, believed what God said, and worshiped God.

WRAP IT UP

Friendship is a relationship, and you can't have a relationship with someone without communicating with him or her. We already have God's communication to us—the Bible. Now what about your communication to God? Understanding reconciliation can transform your devotional and prayer life. Instead of looking at the time you spend with God as something you're *supposed* to do as a Christian or something you *have* to check off your daily to-do list, think about what an amazing privilege it is for you to have this friendship with God!

Without Christ, you couldn't come into God's presence and talk to Him. You'd have no desire to learn about Him or please Him. You'd still hate Him and be His enemy. When you look at your relationship with God with a heart overflowing with gratitude for your reconciliation to Him through Christ, it sheds a new light on spending time with Him. Just like it's not a chore to hang out with your earthly friends, it can be a delight to be with your heavenly friend, but only if you have the right perspective about reconciliation. Earthly friends will move in and out of your life, but God will always be the best friend you could ever have.

How are you doing on your end of the friendship?

DEFINING TRUTH:
Your security for peace and friendship with God is Christ.

This whole section has been about our relationship to God because of Christ; not until the next section will we really cover our interactions with people. However, whenever we learn something about God, it shows us how He wants us to relate to others. So in the Put Off, Renew, and Put On sections, we'll apply our peace and reconciliation with God to our relationship to Him as well as our friendships with others.

Studying God's character shows us what we're supposed to be like. We'll never be a perfect friend like God is, but has the Lord revealed anything in your life that you need to change to be a better earthly friend?

I tend to run to my human friends with my problems, instead of running to my all-powerful, all-loving Friend. I can also care more about what my human friends think about me than about what my heavenly Friend thinks. How can knowing that God is your best friend affect the way you interact with your earthly friends? Agree with God about your sin, and ask for His forgiveness. Then, let's see how you can go about changing!

God is totally sufficient for you. Even if you're going through some friend-related struggle right now, you can be confident that you will always have the best friend you could ever ask for, no matter what you do. Maybe this encourages your heart because in your school you feel rejected by everyone around you because you've tried to take a stand. Maybe this gives you courage to do the right thing if you're involved with some friends that you know you shouldn't be, and you just can't imagine your life without them. Maybe you're just too focused on your friends and spending time with them or pleasing them. How does knowing that God is your constant Friend help you right now in your specific situation with your earthly friends?

PUT OFF

1. Confess it and get rid of it

Has God revealed any sin in your life in your attitude or actions about your friendship with Him? What, specifically?

_____

_____

2. Deal with it

Is there anyone in your life, besides God, to whom you've been a bad friend that you need to ask for forgiveness?

_____

_____

3. Cut it out

How are you going to make it harder for yourself to go back to the sin you've been convicted about? What's keeping you from your time with God? What influences you not to be a godly friend?

_____

_____

Renew Your Mind

1. Memorize it

Write out the verse that you plan to memorize.

_____

_____

_____

2. Meditate on it

How will this passage help you with your friendships, both with God and with people?

_____

_____

PUT ON

1. Swap it

How can your friendship with God change your friendships with people?

_____

_____

2. Check up on it

Who will you ask to check up on you about your relationship with God and your friendships with others? When will you talk to this person about helping you?

_____

_____

7

God's Child and His Heir

You know that annoying conversation kids have when they start comparing everything with their friends and trying to one-up them?

"My dad works at a bank."

"Well, my dad is the *president* of a bank."

"Oh yeah? My dad can lift 250 pounds."

"But, my dad can lift 250 pounds with one hand."

"Well, my dad could lift it with one hand while he runs circles around your dad . . ."

And on and on.

I don't want to say that we're one-upping the truths we're learning about who we are in Christ with each chapter, but we're certainly building on each one. One truth isn't better than another, but there is definitely a progression into more personal territory. The term *justification* talks about our legal standing with God, which is amazing! Then we saw that we went from an enemy of God to His friend, which tells us we have a relationship with Him. *Now* we're looking at adoption and inheritance, which is obviously an even closer relationship than a friendship. It's family!

Let's start by looking at the word *adoption.*

Picture This

Adoption has become more meaningful to my family recently. My brother and sister-in-law are in the process of adopting a little one from Thailand. It's a ton of work and a very draining process. We've been able to see pictures of this precious little boy, and it's starting to become real. As I've studied our adoption in Christ, the whole process has likewise started to become more alive.

Adoption is a big step for a family to take. The whole family dynamic will change. Their little boy won't be a baby, so it could take a long time for him to warm up to us and accept us as his family. He might even be afraid of his new family at first. There will be a huge culture shock when he moves to America, not to mention a language barrier. My brother's family will have to readjust their schedules to having a very young child again, as their other son is already seven years old. They'll have to figure out how to best show love to a new little stranger—now their son—and so will the rest of us aunts and uncles and grandmas and grandpas. They'll have to make sure to spend lots of time with the son they already have, as he learns to accept his new little brother. Their new boy will be at all of our family gatherings from now on and will assume their last name.

It's a big deal to bring someone who is not in your family into your family. I have no doubt that there will be more than enough love to go around, but there will certainly be a time of adjustment to such a huge change.

The truth is that all of us are adopted. We weren't originally born into God's family. We were born to the family of sin and Satan.

READ ALL ABOUT IT

For ye have not received the spirit of bondage again to fear; but ye have received the Spirit of adoption, whereby we cry, Abba, Father. The Spirit itself beareth witness with our spirit, that we are the children of God: and if children, then heirs; heirs of God, and joint-heirs with Christ; if so be that we suffer with him, that we may be also glorified together. (Romans 8:15–17)

But when the fulness of the time was come, God sent forth his Son, made of a woman, made under the law, to redeem them that were under the law, that we might receive the adoption of sons. And because ye are sons, God hath sent forth the Spirit of his Son into your hearts, crying, Abba, Father. Wherefore thou art no more a servant, but a son; and if a son, then an heir of God through Christ. (Galatians 4:4–7)

What's It Mean?

Hey, look! There are some familiar words in those verses: *slave* and *slavery*, which we studied when we learned that Christ ransomed us. This verse completes the picture for us. Not only did Christ buy us out of slavery, freeing us from Satan, but God also adopted us. It's already a huge deal for someone to pay the purchase price to free a slave from bondage, but to also adopt that slave is basically unheard of!

Read John 1:12. Who is responsible for putting us in the position of being able to be adopted? (You may have to look back at the beginning of the chapter to see who it's talking about.)

Let that sink in. Remember, a slave has no rights, no position, and no inheritance. But, after we receive Christ, we're adopted, and we become God's sons (or daughters!) and heirs.

What's It Mean to You?

First, we're God's children. In Romans 8:15, what do you think it means that we can *cry* to God, our Father?

_____

_____

As slaves to Satan, we didn't have the privilege of coming and talking to God in prayer. But as God's children, we can come into His presence and talk to Him whenever we want. One of the benefits of being adopted is that you have an even closer relationship with God than you did just by being reconciled to Him; now He's not only your friend, He's your Father. Do you realize what a privilege it is for a former slave to talk to God as her father? Are you taking advantage of that *privilege* and talking to your Father often?

Read Romans 7:4 and Philippians 3:12. What two phrases do you find in those verses that indicate God's ownership of you?

_____

_____

What's different about how Satan owned you and the way you now belong to God?

_____

_____

We have so much to thank our heavenly Father for!
Now let's look at our *inheritance.*
Here we go one-upping again. As if it's not enough that God saved us out of slavery, made us His friends, and then adopted us, He also made us coheirs with Christ. This means we get the same share of God's inheritance as His only Son, Jesus Christ.

In Bible times, only the firstborn son got the full inheritance and the blessing from the father. That's why it was such a big deal that Esau sold his birthright to Jacob and that Jacob later stole the firstborn blessing from Esau. If things had gone the way they normally did, Esau would have gotten everything from his father Isaac, and Jacob would've basically dropped off the scene. It was a big deal for a father to adopt another son, but to put him on the same level as the firstborn son would've been unthinkable. Yet this is exactly what God did for us. And guess who made all of this possible? Yep, the firstborn Son Himself!

There are two parts to the inheritance we get as an heir of God: the part we get to enjoy here on earth and the part that's waiting for us after death.

Read Psalm 16:5–6 and Numbers 18:20. What is our inheritance on earth?

_____

_____

Have you ever thought about God like that? As believers, we have the Holy Spirit living inside of us, we have access to God, and we have numerous blessings in Christ. What more could we possibly want or need? God is truly our beautiful inheritance, and yet we often struggle with discontentment with what we have or don't have and how our lives are turning out. If only our focus were fixed on this amazing inheritance that we already possess here on earth, just think of how our discontentment would fade!

READ ALL ABOUT IT

Ephesians 1:3 says, "Blessed be the God and Father of our Lord Jesus Christ, who hath blessed us with all spiritual blessings in heavenly places in Christ." Note our key phrase tucked in that verse: *in Christ*. Christ is the one who made all of these spiritual blessings possible. Christ is the one who covered us with His righteousness so that we could be accepted by the Father and adopted as His own.

What's It Mean?

Ephesians 1:3–12 tells us some of the inheritance we received immediately at salvation. Record each one of the blessings we have in Christ that you find in those verses. Prepare to be amazed!

Ephesians 1:4

_____

_____

Ephesians 1:5–6

_____

_____

Ephesians 1:7–8

_____

_____

Ephesians 1:9–10

_____

_____

Ephesians 1:11–12

_____

_____

We're spiritual billionaires! And those are just some of our blessings, just the ones that Paul chose to talk about in this small portion of just one of his letters.

What's It Mean to You?

Meditate on what it's like to be an heir with Christ because God adopted you.

But wait, there's more! Not only do you already possess God as your Father and everything that He is, but one day we will inherit heaven. Remember, we became united with Christ when we accepted His gift of salvation. We became identified with Him, and all the things that are true of Him are true of us. He died, so we died; He was resurrected, so we're resurrected; He is righteous, so we're righteous. And here's another huge blessing: He's God's Son, so we're children of God; He's going to dwell in heaven forever, so we will too.

List some things you know about heaven.

_____

_____

WRAP IT UP

All of that is yours, guaranteed, because of Christ! How amazing is it that a girl who was once a slave to sin and a daughter of Satan can now inherit heaven and all its riches? Who are you? You're an heiress. But just like being an heiress here on earth, it has nothing to do with anything *you* did. Paris Hilton is rolling in the dough because of the empire her family built. She didn't lift a finger to gain all that wealth; she just receives it because of her last name. And you and I have no rights to heaven on our own; we receive the benefits of who our Father is. And remember, He wasn't even originally our Father—He adopted us. We wouldn't have even had a chance at this inheritance if He hadn't initiated it. You can be confident in your inheritance and who you are as an heiress of God, while at the same time being deeply humbled by the fact that it has nothing to do with you.

Write a prayer or some thoughts expressing gratefulness to God for adopting you and making you an heir with Christ.

_____

_____

What characteristics will people see in your life if you're constantly meditating on your adoption and your inheritance?

_____

_____

[
DEFINING TRUTH:
Your security for present and future blessing is Christ.

PUT OFF

1. Confess it and get rid of it

Ask the Lord to forgive you for your sinful attitudes and to help transform you into a thankful child and heiress.

_____

_____

2. Deal with it

What do you need to do to show your gratitude to God for all that He's done for you?

_____

_____

3. Cut it out

What do you need to cut out of your life to make it harder for you to go back to your sinful thoughts or actions?

_____

_____

Renew Your Mind

1. Memorize it

Write out the verse that you plan to memorize.

_____

_____

_____

2. Meditate on it

How will this passage help you remain grateful for your adoption by God?

_____

_____

_____

PUT ON

1. Swap it

What attitudes and actions do you need to put on in place of your sinful ones?

_____

_____

2. Check up on it

Who can you ask to keep you accountable about your responses to your adoption by God? (You can ask a friend to catch you if you are negative or ungrateful since they're probably the ones you complain to most often!) When will you talk to this person about helping you?

_____

_____

8 Loved by God
No Matter What

ove is one of the most talked-about emotions in our society. We all love to be loved. A phrase you hear quite often right now is that you have to "learn to love yourself." The world continually says that every problem you have from obesity to depression to immorality comes from not loving or respecting yourself enough. I heard a new one the other day. A lady said she needed to learn how to be there for herself. Huh? Figure that one out. How are you ever *not there* for yourself?

All of the low self-esteem jargon stems from this kind of thinking. People would say that insecurities, like the ones with which I've always struggled, come from a lack of love for myself. I should just accept that I'm awesome and talented and beautiful, and if people have a problem with me. . . well, whatever. This is how I am.

> *Jesus said unto him, Thou shalt love the Lord thy God with all thy heart, and with all thy soul, and with all thy mind. This is the first and great commandment. And the second is like unto it, Thou shalt love thy neighbour as thyself.* (Matthew 22:37–39)

We're commanded to love God and love others. Unless I'm missing it, there's not a third command to love ourselves. What's implied by the phrase "love your neighbor *as yourself*"?

_____

_____

We all love ourselves too much, plain and simple. Yet the world says you need to learn to love your looks and flaunt your body (even if you don't think you're beautiful), even when God says that you're not to think of yourself in a proud way (Romans 12:3). The world says you should be confident in your personality or abilities, when God says that our confidence should be in the work of Jesus Christ (Ephesians 3:11, 12). The world will get it wrong every time, so we need to go to the source of wisdom to define who we are.

You don't need to learn to love yourself. You *do* need to learn to love God and love others. And there's one more thing you need to know and never doubt: you are loved by God. Hang with me; we're not going into the touchy-feely territory. We're dealing with the honest truth here. It's a fact that God loves you.

Sometimes we really do need encouragement. Life can be discouraging. Relationships can be discouraging. Where we turn for that encouragement is what matters. We shouldn't turn to everyone around us, grasping for love and approval. We also shouldn't turn inward and try to build ourselves up. We need to turn upward to our heavenly Father.

READ ALL ABOUT IT

Let's go to a familiar but intensely awesome passage. Read Romans 8:31–39.

What's It Mean?

I'll look up some of the words in verse 35 for you, and you look up the ones I've left blank.

separate (5563)—to place any room between
love (26)—affection, benevolence, a love-feast
tribulation (2347)

_____

distress (4730)

_____

persecution (1375)—oppressive treatment
famine (3042)—destitution, hunger
nakedness (1132)—nudity
peril (2794)

_____

sword (3162)—judicial punishment; war
Using the definitions we found, write Romans 8:35 in your own words.

_____

_____

_____

Verse 35 raises a question that the rest of the passage in Romans 8:31–39 answers. Who can separate or put any room whatsoever between you and the love of Christ?

_____

_____

Love here means "everlasting affection" or "kindness." I enjoy one of the pictures _Strong's_ gives: love-feast. The word _meal_ makes me think of some food sitting on a dining room table. The word _feast_ makes me think of mountains of food covering every inch of dozens of enormous tables. This is

Christ's love for us—a mountain of never-ending, completely satisfying, affectionate, kind love.

Paul then goes on to describe all kinds of situations and asks if they separate us from God's love: pressure, trouble, hopelessness that feels like the walls are closing in, situations that offer no way out, anguish of spirit, lack of food or clothes, persecution, danger, and war. In verse 37, he answers his question: "Can any of those things separate us from God's love? No!" Even in all these worst-case scenarios, we emerge as conquerors—more than conquerors—because of who or what?

_____

Just in case he forgot anything in the first list, Paul adds everything and everyone else he can think of to Romans 8:38–39, and repeats that *none* of them can put any distance between us and God's love.

I love the phrase at the very end of verse 39 that wraps up his argument. Nothing can separate us from the love of God which is *in whom*?

_____

There's our study phrase again. Because of Christ, we have access to this never-ending love! From John 3:16, we know that God loves the whole world, but for those of us *in Christ*, we will never be parted from this love of God. We'll spend eternity with Him in His loving presence forever, because of Christ. That's why verse 38 assures us that even death can't put any room between God and us; death only takes us into the very presence of the one who loves us.

What's It Mean to You?

Have you ever gone through a time where you felt like nobody loved you? Describe why you felt this way.

_____

_____

How did you respond to feeling unloved? How did it affect your mood?

_____

_____

The fact is that when we feel like nobody loves us, we're actually believing a lie. Romans 8 tells us that there is always Someone who loves us, no matter what. Nothing can change that love; no one can alter it; it is always true 100 percent of every moment of every day for your whole life on earth and in eternity. You can't add to or detract from that love even though you don't deserve it.

You may have a hard time believing this is true because, when we look for love, we often want the world's version of love. We want to *feel* it and *experience* it in some tangible way. When you described the day that you didn't think anyone acted in a loving way toward you, you probably mentioned something about your friends ignoring you or not complimenting you or even teasing you in hurtful way. You might have said something about a teacher or your parents being unfair. Someone might have forgotten some important event in your life, or maybe you just had a bad day and none of your loved ones picked up on it. Maybe you failed at something and felt terrible about it, and no one encouraged you. Whatever it was, you just didn't get the *feeling* that anyone cared about you.

There will be times in your life when the bottom falls out of your world. Whether real or imagined, you will go through times that you don't get the impression that everyone around you adores you. If you're living your life looking for love and acceptance from people, and if you base your joy and fulfillment on this love, you *will* be disappointed and insecure. That's not to say that you won't have wonderful, loving relationships with people, but that can't be your primary focus. People will fail you and will never love you perfectly, just like you'll fail them and never love them perfectly. But nothing and no one can ever separate you from the perfect love of your heavenly Father.

Why? Because you're so beautiful and talented and perfect? Because you deserve it? Not so much. How can you know you'll always have God's love?

_____

_____

If you said something like, "Because He said so," you're right. But sometimes we have a hard time believing what God says, even though we shouldn't. Want even more proof? Here it is: because "I know that God loves His Son."[1]

That's our claim to God's never-ending love. That's why Romans 8:39 ends with a reminder that we're in Christ. Because He is the reason we can *never* be separated from God's love.

On days when you're fighting discouragement and feeling like you've hit rock bottom, fight Satan's lies that nobody loves you. On good days when you feel loved and accepted by others, don't forget about the most important one, who loves you perfectly, always.

In our society, where we think of love as a feeling instead of a fact, it's sometimes hard for us to believe God actually loves us. This is especially true when circumstances in our lives aren't going the way we want; it's particularly hard to believe that God, who's in control of those circumstances and is allowing them to happen to us, still loves us. "How can He love me and allow *this* in my life?" This is when we have to turn again to facts, not feelings.

Let's build up a list of hard evidence about God's love for you, so you can preach truth to yourself the next time you doubt God's love.

Read the following verses and, in the blanks provided, write the evidence of God's love that you found in the verse.

Behold, for peace I had great bitterness: but thou hast in love to my soul delivered it from the pit of corruption: for thou hast cast all my sins behind thy back. (Isaiah 38:17)

The Lord hath appeared of old unto me, saying, Yea, I have loved thee with an everlasting love: therefore with loving-kindness have I drawn thee. (Jeremiah 31:3)

But the very hairs of your head are all numbered. Fear ye not therefore, ye are of more value than many sparrows. (Matthew 10:30, 31)

But God commendeth his love toward us, in that, while we were yet sinners, Christ died for us. (Romans 5:8)

Behold, what manner of love the Father hath bestowed upon us, that we should be called the sons of God: therefore the world knoweth us not, because it knew him not. (1 John 3:1)

Hereby perceive we the love of God, because he laid down his life for us: and we ought to lay down our lives for the brethren. (1 John 3:16)

In this was manifested the love of God toward us, because that God sent his only begotten Son into the world, that we might live through him. Herein is love, not that we loved God, but that he loved us, and sent his Son to be the propitiation for our sins. (1 John 4:9–10)

That he would grant you, according to the riches of his glory, to be strengthened with might by his Spirit in the inner man; That Christ may dwell in your hearts by faith; that ye, being rooted and grounded in love, May be able to comprehend with all saints what is the breadth, and length, and depth, and height; And to know the love of Christ, which passeth knowledge, that ye might be filled with all the fulness of God. (Ephesians 3:16–19)

As many as I love, I rebuke and chasten: be zealous therefore, and repent. (Revelation 3:19)

There are tons of verses about characteristics of God's love and many others that prove He loves us. In fact, love is the most often-mentioned attribute of God in the Bible. A study just about His love for you will keep you busy for a long time!

What is the one thing that God did for you that is the only piece of evidence you should ever need to prove, without a doubt, that He loves you?

If a friend or family member literally sacrificed his or her life so that you could live, and someone asked you if you thought the person who died for you really loved you, can you imagine shrugging and saying, "I don't know. I don't really *feel* loved"? That would be crazy! There is no greater proof of love than offering your life for someone else's.

We know that Christ came from heaven into the world, out of love for us, died specifically for our sins so that we could live forever with Him, rose again, and is coming back to get us someday; but because that was thousands of years ago and we never saw Jesus, we don't *feel* like He really loves us. We even complain, question God, mope around, and desperately seek love and approval from others. We choose to believe, against all evidence, that God doesn't love us.

He has given us more evidence of His love than any human being ever can or will. He's given us life; He sustains our every breath; He gives us good gifts; He disciplines us when we sin; He allows us to have a relationship with Him; He knows everything about us; He gives us so much more than we deserve; and most importantly, He sent His only Son to die for us to rescue our souls from hell, and then He gave us peace with Him and adopted us into His family! How much more evidence of His love do we need? You can't name anyone on earth who has done all that for you; I don't care how loved that person makes you *feel*!

"God loves you so much that he sent his Son to suffer for sin, the righteous for the unrighteous, so that he might bring you to himself! Is this the action of someone who isn't filled with fervent love for you?"[2]

WRAP IT UP

On the days that you feel left out, unloved, unaccepted, or unpopular, remember the Friend who is "for you," like it says in Romans 8:31. With God on your side, it doesn't matter who is against you. He already gave His own Son to die for you (8:32), and He assures you that nothing can ever change His love for you. He will never love you more or less than He does right now. No one can ever separate you from His love, not here on earth, not after you die. The more you study about how awesome your God is the more this begins to mean to you. If you have the love of this amazing God, what more do you need?

Usually, when we feel like no one loves us, we're just imagining it. There probably is at least one human somewhere in the world who will always love you. But let's just pretend you're right and no one on earth loves you. God does. And His love is all you need.

Here are some points to remember next time you're discouraged and feel unloved:

1. God loves you.

2. His love for you is secure because it's based on His Son.

3. People's love for you will change; God's never will!

When you're discouraged, you can mediate on God's everlasting, never-changing love for you. But what about when you're struggling to love God and others as you should? These two commands give most of us a hard time our whole lives. Christ knew what He was doing when He boiled everything down to these two things. It shouldn't be hard for us to love God, unless we never take time to think about who He is and all that He's done for us. When we neglect to meditate on His incredible love, having a relationship with Him turns into a duty instead of a natural outpouring of love in response to His love for us. The answer to loving God as you should, loving others as you should, and *not* loving yourself like you naturally do comes down to meditating on God's mind-blowing love for you.

We need to take a long, hard look at God's love for us, and then ask Him to change our natural tendency to love only ourselves and to give us His supernatural love. When we truly meditate on who He is, He can produce the same kind of love for Him and others in our lives. Many Christians take the awesome fact that God loves them and build up their self-esteem with it, thinking, "I'm so good, God loves me. I'm so worth it, God died for me. I'm beautiful, so God can't help but love me." But, yet again, God's love has nothing to do with us and everything to do with who He is. His incredible kindness toward disgusting, horrible sinners like us inspires praise and love back to Him. How can we not love someone who has given everything to us?

Studying God's overwhelming, sacrificial love for proud, stubborn, hopeless sinners like us also inspires us to have sacrificial love for the proud, stubborn, unlovable people around us. The world will tell you that you can "fall out of love" with people. And that's very true . . . if love is just a feeling. But God's kind of love is a choice. God's kind of love is directed toward people who were His enemies (you and me) and doesn't change based on how loveable we are (not at all). It's a great rebuke when you just don't feel like "loving your neighbor as yourself"! Let His love for you burrow into your heart and fill it to overflowing, and then it will pour out in love for Him and other people.

[**DEFINING TRUTH:**
Your secure place in God's never-ending love is Christ.

So how does knowing that God loves you define who you are?

_____

_____

When you feel like no one loves you, what truth/fact do you need to preach to yourself?

_____

_____

Is there anything you can do to make that fact more true than it already is?

_____

Do you deserve God's love?

_____

What does that tell you about God?

_____

_____

What does that tell you about yourself?

_____

_____

Does knowing that God loves you even though you don't deserve it make you care more or less about whether or not you feel like people love and accept you?

_____

Why?

_____

_____

When you're discouraged or have had a rotten day, what should you meditate on to change your gloominess into thankfulness?

_____

_____

How does knowing about God's love give you the right kind of humble confidence about who you are?

_____

_____

When someone is hard to love, what do you need to meditate on to help you learn to love them more?

_____

_____

How does knowing about God's love for you help you love other people (even if they don't deserve it)?

_____

_____

PUT OFF

1. Confess it and get rid of it

Have you doubted God's love for you recently? Is there a specific person (people) you're struggling with loving right now? Identify those sins and ask the Lord's forgiveness.

_____

_____

2. Deal with it

Is there a person (besides God) from whom you need to seek forgiveness for your lack of love for them?

_____

_____

3. Cut it out

What do you need to cut out of your life to help you love God and others more?

_____

_____

Renew Your Mind

1. Memorize it

Write out the verse that you plan to memorize.

_____

_____

_____

2. Meditate on it

How will this passage help you love God and others?

_____

_____

PUT ON

1. Swap it

What practical actions do you need to begin doing to show love to others as a result of God's love for you?

_____

_____

2. Check up on it

Who can you ask to keep you accountable to grow in love? When will you talk to this person about helping you?

_____

_____

9
Not My Own Person

This is one of the most defining and life-changing principles we'll cover in this whole study. In this chapter, you'll see not only who you are, but also your entire purpose in life. "So, why wasn't this the first chapter in the book?" you may ask. Well, it's the same reason all of the chapters about how you interact with people come after all the chapters about what God has done for you. Just like you need motivation to love people as God loves you, you need motivation to want to glorify God with your life. There are entire books written on this topic, so obviously, we're going to barely skim the surface, but you can excavate more on your own later.

Picture This

We have all probably been asked at some point in our lives what we want to be when we grow up. When I was little, I changed my mind almost monthly. If it was time for the winter Olympics, I wanted to be a figure skater and would spend hours twirling in a tutu and completing dazzling (almost) double spins on my bedroom carpet. During the summer

Olympics, I decided to be a gymnast; although, about the only move I could even pretend to do was the wave and nod to the judges to signify my performance was about to start. In kindergarten I wanted to be a nurse, regardless of the fact that I couldn't stand the sight of blood. That dream didn't die until I discovered a nurse has to be logical, scientific, and calm under pressure—definitely, not me. Later I wanted to be an artist, then an author, then a teacher, and then an actress.

Most of you are at a stage in your life where you can discern your strengths, gifts, and desires. You may even be in college or soon will be, and you are thinking about what field of study you want to pursue. You might actually define yourself based on your gifts. "I play the piano." "I want to be a nurse." "I think I want to teach." "I'm into sports." You may spend hours every week practicing and pursuing your passion. You can probably fill in this blank without needing to think for very long: "I want to_____."

Write a brief description of what you want to do with your life at this point.

_____

_____

Reread your answer above. How would your life be different if you filled in that space with, "I want my life to glorify God, my Creator, no matter what?" Am I saying that if you wrote, "I want to work with autistic children" or "I want to get married and coach high school basketball" that you should be ashamed of yourself? Of course not. But we're seeking to discover who we are as Christian young women, and the principle that most defines us is this: we were created in Christ to glorify God. Period. That's it. That's why we're on this earth!

If you actually take the time to think about that and really try to wrap your mind around it, this should be a very sobering thought. This principle should affect how we live, make decisions, and interact with other people.

READ ALL ABOUT IT

Read the following passages: Revelations 4:11, Colossians 1:16–17, and 1 Corinthians 10:31. How do these verses fit together?

_____

_____

What's It Mean?

Now go back to Revelations 4:11. Let's look up each word in a concordance. I'll do some for you to read and you do some. Write the definition for each word.

Thou art worthy, O Lord, to receive glory and honour and power: for thou hast created all things, and for thy pleasure they are and were created. (Revelation 4:11)

worthy (514)

_____

Lord (2962)—supreme in authority, controller, He to whom a person or thing belongs, about which He has power of deciding; master, lord, the possessor and disposer of a thing, the owner; one who has control of the person, the master

to receive (2983)—to take what is one's own, to take with the hand, lay hold of any person or thing in order to use it

glory (1391)

_____

honour (5092)

_____

power (1411)—miraculous power; ability, abundance, might, strength

hast created (2936)

_____

thy pleasure (2307)—God's purpose, desire, will

Keeping in mind all the definitions you just discovered, rewrite Revelation 4:11 in your own words.

_____

_____

_____

One of the main things to get out of this verse is the definition of the word *Lord*. The very essence of this word describes God as master, the supreme authority, and the controller. Since He owns something, He can do with it whatever He wants to do. And the thing He owns is you!

What's It Mean to You?

So here's another nugget that defines you as a Christian young woman: You are not your own person. You belong to God because He created you.

Why did He create you, according to Revelation 4:11?

_____

You've probably heard before now that you were created for God's glory. The word in Revelation 4:11 is His *pleasure.* We think of pleasure as happiness or enjoyment. And that's partly why God created us, but the Greek definition of that word is "for His purpose or His will." We're not on earth for any other reason than to do His will and give Him glory. If we're honest, that's not how we go about living most days of our life. See if you can recognize yourself in any of the following situations.

- When you desperately seek approval from other people and change how you act or look to get that approval, you're not living as if God and His glory are the only things that matter.
- When you've decided that you're going to a certain college to major in whatever you want, regardless of whether

it's the best place for you to grow and learn to use your skills for God, you're acting like you don't care that God is your Master and owner.

- When you get obsessed with a TV show, a boy, a friend, how you look, a sport, or an activity and neglect your time with the Lord, you're living like it doesn't matter that the Lord who created you wants to have a relationship with you so that you can learn how to bring Him more glory.

- When you're with a group of people, worrying about what they think of you, you're unable to think of the ways you can bring God glory through your interactions with those people.

- When you're constantly talking about yourself, seeking to be the center of attention, and sulking or getting angry when people don't treat you the way you think you deserve to be treated, you're more concerned about your glory than you are about God's.

Any time you decide that you want to live to please yourself or other people instead of doing what God wants, you're going directly against the entire reason you were created. You're acting like you belong to yourself. But you don't.

This is our purpose in life—glorifying God. This defines who we are. So, off you go, girls! Go glorify God with your lives.

Not that simple, is it? We'd better figure out exactly *how* we're supposed to bring Him glory.

What's It Mean?

In his commentary on Ephesians, John MacArthur says, "It is from *poiēma* (workmanship) that we get poem, a piece of literary workmanship. Before time began, God designed us to be conformed to the image of his Son, Jesus Christ."[1]

In your opinion, what makes a good poem or story?

A good work of literature allows you to get lost in the imagery it creates. It allows readers to experience some emotion or picture something in a way they never would have before reading it. When a poem, book, or work of art inspires you in some way, you probably look to see who wrote it or created it, so if anyone ever asks you who your favorite author or artist is, you'll know at least one name to give. Let's say you read *A Tale of Two Cities*, and then tell someone that your favorite author is Charles Dickens. What did you just do? You just gave glory to the author because you appreciated his creation.

We are God's work of art. Through our lives, we have the opportunity to showcase how amazing He is. But that still doesn't tell us how to do that exactly, so let's keep going.

We are created *in Christ*. There are two ways to take this. First, Christ was literally involved in creation. He was there when we were created and part of the creation process, like it says in Colossians 1:16: "For by **him** were all things created, that are in heaven, and that are in earth, visible and invisible, . . . all things were created by him, and for him." Christ was also responsible for our creation as new creatures. It says in 2 Corinthians 5:17: "Therefore if any man be **in Christ**, he is a new creature: old things are passed away; behold, all things are become new." One of the meanings of this word *created* is "completely transformed." When we were saved, we were transformed into another person because of Christ. So the only way we can possibly glorify God is because of our new creation through Christ.

Here's another verse to think about.

> For we are His workmanship created in Christ Jesus unto good works, which God hath before ordained that we should walk in them. (Ephesians 2:10)

We're going to focus on the phrase "that we should walk." We'll come back to the "them" in a minute. The phrase *should walk* means "to live or conduct your entire life." So as God's work of art, we should live our entire life doing . . . doing what? Doing "good works." I found a truckload of words that mean *good*. Here are a few: *useful, pleasant, excellent, upright, honorable*, and *joyful*.

As for *works*, the idea is toil or a labor. Brace yourself for a big surprise here: the emphasis is on working rather than doing anything that isn't work. Obviously, right? The point is that these useful, pleasant, honorable, excellent deeds aren't always things we enjoy doing or that come naturally to us. They take work.

Picture This

In our family budget, we have a ministry category to give gifts to missionary speakers, to provide a meal for a sick family, or to help someone who's going through a rough time. My husband teases me because I tend to get into the habit of cheating with this category. If my personal budgeted funds run out and a friend wants to go for coffee, I let that fall under *ministry* because I'm sure we'll encourage each other spiritually or because I'll pay for her coffee in order to *minister* to her. Michael informed me that going to Starbucks and yacking with a friend for three hours is not the purpose of our ministry category. And he's right. (Sigh.)

Can you do a good work for someone whom you love and enjoy helping? Absolutely. However, we should also make a habit of showing love to unlovable people or doing something that would really cost us time, effort, or money even if no one even knows that we did it. This would be a true good work.

Why should we do these good works? To make God love us more? To help contribute to our salvation? So other people will think we're good girls? Nope. Ephesians 2:10 comes right after Ephesians 2:8–9, which we studied earlier.

What do those verses say that works *don't* do?

_____

_____

Verse 10 reveals that works are part of God's plan for His new, saved creatures. Good works don't save us, but they are the result of a transformed life. God planned before time (that's what *ordained* means) that this was how we should live to bring glory to our Creator.

Read John 15:8. What do good works (fruit) show others?

_____

_____

Good works are a natural outpouring of a growing Christian who has a relationship with God. We will bear the fruit of good works if we are truly saved. Some Christians will bear more fruit, but every true Christian will produce some fruit. When our life is full of excellent, useful, and joyful deeds that aren't necessarily easy, we're like a beautiful poem or work of art that points to God and says, "Isn't He amazing. Look what He's doing through me." We've already seen that on our own we can do no good, so any good in our life has to be because of Him.

WRAP IT UP

How do we produce these good works? We know they're hard to do and not something that we can just work up in our own strength. We know we have a hard time fighting our sinful desires, and we can't even do that on our own. So how do we go above and beyond just resisting sin and actually fill our lives with attitudes and actions that please God?

Read Galatians 5:16. Who helps us not live how our flesh wants to live?

What do you think the word *walk* means in that verse? (You can look up number 4043 in *Strong's* for the exact definition.)

In our own strength, we can't glorify God. Left to our-selves, we'll try our best to bring glory to . . . ourselves. Read Galatians 5:19–21 and write down the kind of works we would go back to if we weren't saved by Christ and didn't have the Holy Spirit living inside of us.

Hmm. Those definitely won't glorify God. But what characteristics will be part of our lives if we walk in the Spirit according to Galatians 5:22–23?

Think harder on this one. According to Galatians 5:24, why won't our old desires control us anymore?

It always comes back to Him, doesn't it? Because Christ saved us, we are restored to God's original purpose for creating us. We're able to bring God glory again, where we couldn't before we were saved. As we live our lives, submitting to the Holy Spirit daily, He will work to produce the fruit of the Spirit in us, and our lives can be God's beautiful work of art, pointing to our Creator. Pretty good system, huh?

So instead of adopting the world's attitude of "This is my life; I've only got one, and I'm going to live it up and get the most I can out of it," we need to adopt Christ's attitude: "Not my will but Yours, Oh Lord."

[DEFINING TRUTH:
Your ability to glorify God is found in Christ.

The opposite of giving God glory is trying to bring glory to ourselves. Our natural tendency is to live like we belong to ourselves without thinking about Our Creator and Master.

Examine the direction of your life in general and look at particular tendencies or thought patterns you've noticed recently.

Read Romans 1:21–25. This passage is all about idolatry. What is a good definition of idolatry based on verse 25?

_____

_____

If idolatry is worshipping something that was created rather than the One who created it, list at least one way that you were guilty of idolatry this week.

_____

_____

You may have never thought about trying to be accepted by your friends or being proud of your accomplishments as idolatry before, but it is. We're all guilty of it at one point or other. It's a sin, and it's disgusting to God. We have to put off our sin, change our mindset by using God's Word, and put on different actions that will lift up God, not ourselves or other people.

Ask the Lord to forgive you for these sins of glorifying others or yourself, instead of Him. Commit to getting these sinful tendencies out of your life.

PUT OFF

1. Confess it and get rid of it

In what specific areas have you been living for your own glory (thinking that you deserve praise, maybe even worship) instead of God's? Look back at the list on page 106–7.

_____

_____

2. Deal with it

Is there anyone besides God that you've affected by your sin and from whom you need to seek forgiveness?

_____

_____

3. Cut it out

What specific things do you need to cut out of your life to make it harder for you to be tempted to bring glory to yourself or to put people higher than God?

_____

_____

Renew Your Mind

1. Memorize it

Write out the verse that you plan to memorize.

_____

_____

_____

2. Meditate on it

How will this passage help you live for God's glory?

_____

_____

_____

PUT ON

1. Swap it

With what godly thoughts and actions do you need to replace your old sinful thoughts and actions?

_____

_____

2. Check up on it

Who will you ask to check up on you and keep you accountable about this particular sin struggle? When will you talk to this person about helping you?

_____

_____

SECTION 3
Who Am I in Relation to Other People?

10 Made to Please God, Not People

f you're anything like I was as a teenager or college student, you might've flipped through the table of contents, found that this section sounded most interesting, and skipped over the other two sections to start here. (You know who you are. Take this as your official shooing back to whatever chapter you're supposed to be on.) There are just some topics that have a greater draw for young women. For me it was always guys, friends, dating, marriage, or just about anything about relationships with people in general. I wouldn't have been very excited to have to wade through *justification* and *reconciliation* before I could finally get to the juicy stuff.

I purposefully put this section toward the end because true understanding of how we are to relate to people comes after true understanding of how we relate to God. There may be fewer verses that actually contain the phrase *in Christ* in this section. Yet everything we're about to study about how to relate to people comes from what we've already learned about who we are in Christ. Be on the lookout for principles we've studied that apply in this section. Trust me, they're there. This is not a fun chapter. As I worked through it, I discovered it's much more of an "ouch" chapter than I originally thought it would be.

It's true that people are very important. We are on this earth to bring glory to God, and one of the primary ways we do this is either by reaching other people with the gospel if they're unsaved or by ministering God's Word and His love to our fellow Christians. There's a big difference between this view of people's importance and (sadly) our usual view of people as the all-important beings who make or break our life by their acceptance or rejection.

As a teenager and through college, I knew I struggled with this. I even started a notebook of verses about how God is more than enough for me. I filled the pages with His many commands to please Him, not people. This was the beginning of the growth process for me. Exposure to God's Word is always good and helpful, but I was trying to just magically change my actions by throwing verses at my problem without focusing on the root of it—my heart. I wanted to please God, but I still longed for people's approval, and more often than not, people's approval won out over God's. It wasn't until I started to really learn who I am in Christ that the verses about not pleasing people began to fall into their proper place.

READ ALL ABOUT IT

Let's start by reading James 2:1. James begins by commanding that if you're a Christian, you shouldn't need everything you possess in Christ plus favoritism or partiality toward people. List some of the things we have in Christ that we've studied so far.

_____

_____

Based on what you know about Christ, why do you think that being partial toward certain people over other people doesn't fit with that list?

_____

_____

James takes it one step further in verses 9 and 10. Skip down and read those. What does he say about the person who favors certain people over others?

_____

_____

That's pretty harsh, right? It's easy to think of pleasing people as a minor sin or one that doesn't really hurt anyone. But James, inspired by God, says that this is a sin just as big as any other sin. In fact, what are the next two examples in verse 11 that he gives of a person who is just as guilty?

_____

_____

It's obviously not a little sin in God's eyes.

What's It Mean?

Turn to the following passages and write out some of the characteristics you would find in a person whose goal is to please others.

James 2:2–4

_____

_____

1 Samuel 15:24

_____

_____

Matthew 6:1–18

_____

_____

John 12:43

_____

_____

Jude 1:16

_____

_____

What's It Mean to You?

Ask yourself if you see any of these traits in your own life. Really examine your heart and actions, and try not to just fly through these questions.

Do you have a desire to be seen with or liked by attractive or popular people? If so, who is the person (or people) that you're trying to imitate or from whom you want to gain favor?

_____

_____

How are you trying to get their approval?

_____

_____

Do you fear (literally _hold in awe or reverence_) any person? If so, who?

_____

_____

Do you want to please them so badly that you're willing to listen to them (or obey them) like Saul did, rather than listening to God?

_____

_____

What specific things are you doing to please them that might not please God?

_____

_____

Do you accept positions of service in your church, school, home, youth group, or other places so that other people will see you serving and think that you're a *good Christian girl*?

_____

_____

Name the ministries or service opportunities in which you're involved that you tend to participate in so that people will think well of you. (It could be as little as putting money in the offering plate or as public as playing an instrument in church.)

_____

_____

After you've served behind the scenes with no one around, do you try to mention your good deed casually to other people at some point? Name an instance when you have done this recently.

_____

_____

What was your motivation for letting it slip that you did something kind for someone or were asked to serve in some way?

_____

_____

Do you say all the right things when you pray in front of people or put on a spiritual language at church so that others will think you're godly?

_____

_____

What is your motivation for being the first person to volunteer to serve or to answer every question in your Sunday school class?

_____

_____

Have you ever given someone a compliment that you didn't really mean in order to flatter them and make them like you? When have you done this? Is it a continual pattern of your life?

_____

_____

Have you ever used one person to make you look better in front of another person? Name an instance where you have done this recently.

_____

_____

If you answered yes to any of those questions, your actions reveal that you're a people-pleaser, plain and simple. (And let's face it, all of us have done one or more of those things at some point; maybe we even do them continually.) Your heart views people as more important than God. Whether you're a Pleaser or a Confident, most of you seek immediate approval from those around you and adjust your actions accordingly. This attitude reveals an improper view of God; you act like people are important and God is insignificant.

Remember that our purpose is to glorify God, meaning to make Him big or great. When we're people-pleasing, we either make another person's name great or we try to make our own name great in other people's eyes. Again, we go against the whole reason we were created, and we've jumped back into idolatry. Sounds much more serious than "I just want people to like me," doesn't it? As unpleasant as it is, let's call this what it is, girls—sin!

What's It Mean?

Let's look at the opposite of all the characteristics listed above.

In James 2:1–4, we're commanded to not prefer certain people to others because of their wealth, attractiveness, or any gain to us. Romans 2:11 says, "For there is no respect of persons with God." So why shouldn't we show partiality?

_____

_____

That verse is talking about how God judges us. Aren't you glad that how attractive, rich, or popular you are doesn't determine how much He loves you? I know I am.

In 1 Samuel 15:24, Saul confesses that he disobeyed God simply because the people told him to. Saul listened to them even though God had told him to do the opposite. When Saul says he feared the people, he means that he revered them or basically worshiped them. Read the following verses and record why we should fear God rather than fear man.

And fear not them which kill the body, but are not able to kill the soul: but rather fear him which is able to destroy both soul and body in hell. (Matthew 10:28)

_____

_____

Fear ye not the reproach of men, neither be ye afraid of their revilings. For the moth shall eat them up like a garment, and the worm shall eat them like wool: but my righteousness shall be for ever, and my salvation from generation to generation. (Isaiah 51:7–8)

_____

_____

Both the Greek and Hebrew words for *fear* in this instance can mean *reverence* and *awe* or the emotional kind of fear. Either way, God puts it in perspective for us: we have nothing to fear from puny man. The most a person can do is kill us, but God already saved our souls from eternal death, so we have nothing to be afraid of there. And as for being in awe of a person, they're God's creation, just like we are, and will turn back into dirt when they die, just like we will. There's not much to worship there. Maybe instead we should worship the all-powerful, loving, righteous one who has the power to save our souls! OK, not *maybe*. Definitely!

Matthew 6:1–18 is pretty convicting to those of us who've grown up in Christian homes and attended church all of our lives. It's easy to fall into spiritual habits. We know what our parents or spiritual leaders want us to say, so we say it. We know how we're supposed to dress and act and talk at church, so we do it. We know we're supposed to serve, so we serve.

Picture This

I grew up at a Christian camp and started officially working there part-time when I was twelve. In that atmosphere, it was cool to serve. I learned early on that a young person serving with a cheerful attitude impressed people. So that's what I did. I loved working in the public places like the snack shop, bookstore, craft shop, coffee shop, or waitressing. But cleaning toilets, stocking shelves, or working in the back office at a computer . . . not so much. Why? No one even knew I was back there! "What's the point of that?" I wondered.

Obviously, my goal was to serve to be seen. I loved it when people recognized that I was sacrificing to make their camp experience more enjoyable. I didn't love doing the dirty jobs, the kind that make a camp run but never get recognition.

It's easy to do this even now. Maybe we don't like cleaning up after a church fellowship. We'd rather serve the drinks during the fellowship so that everyone knows we're helping. Maybe we enjoy singing in the choir rather than helping in the nursery or being recognized as a spiritual leader rather than helping a hurting friend behind closed doors.

What a rebuke Matthew 6:1–2 is! Who will *not* reward us if we serve only to receive the praise of others?

_____

_____

What is our *only* reward if we do all the right things just to be seen?

_____

_____

What's It Mean to You?

In his commentary, Matthew Henry brings out two interesting and sad points about Matthew 6:2.[1] First, he notes that the praise of men is "their reward," which is not the reward that God intends for those who serve Him. If we do something in front of people so that they'll pat us on the back, like us, or think well of us, and they did all of those things, then we accomplished our goals and got *our* reward, but not God's best reward. The second point Henry notes is that we've already received our reward; it's the only one we're going to get. God longs to give heavenly rewards to His children, but He will not have any reward left to give to us if our reason for serving is not to glorify Him.

Does that mean that if you're participating in some public form of ministry, you should put a bag over your head so no one will know it's you and give you credit for a job well done? Obviously not. (You'd call far more attention to yourself if you did that than if you look normal.)

It all comes down to your heart attitude. If your entire reason for serving is so that people will see you and think you're a great person, you're collecting only earthly rewards. You may get everything you desire at the time, but people's praise won't last. A new person will come along who can play the piano better than you can or who is great at teaching that kids' class, and she'll get all of the attention you used to get. That will be devastating . . . *if* your goal is for people to recognize you.

However, if we serve out of a heart of love for God and a desire to bring Him glory by worshiping Him through serving, we won't care if our service goes completely unnoticed by everyone around us. We're serving for an audience of one, and He will notice. And He'll reward us openly, even if that day doesn't come until we stand before Him in heaven.

I love how the Bible can be so blunt sometimes. Check out John 12:43: "For they loved the praise of men more than the praise of God."

That verse puts everything in perspective for us. When we choose not to follow Christ, but to do whatever is most acceptable to the people around us, we show that we love people and their approval more than God and His approval. Doesn't that sound terrible? But that's what people-pleasing is at its core—choosing the creation over the Creator.

The word *praise* means "glory, honor, or worship." Remember, our purpose is to glorify God, not for other people to glorify us. The context of John 12:43 reveals that many religious leaders in Jesus' day really did believe that He was the Messiah, but they were so scared that the Pharisees would turn on them and shame them that they never publicly talked about their faith. They were concerned the popular religious crowd would reject them.

WRAP IT UP

Have you ever kept quiet about your faith or standards so that you would fit in with those around you? Remind yourself of what happened and why you stayed quiet.

_____

_____

According to Psalm 73:25–26, what should our heart attitude be toward God?

_____

_____

How would that attitude affect the way we respond to other people and their approval?

_____

_____

Jude 1:16 lists some characteristics of false teachers, and the last one in the list is that they show favoritism to certain people to get something for themselves. They tell people whatever they want to hear and use flattery to gain favor. God condemns both flattery and lies in Psalm 12:2–3. Read those verses, and write what you think a double heart means in this case.

_____

_____

Can you think of an example from Jesus' life when He told the truth and refused to flatter people even when it made Him very unpopular?

_____

_____

We should never use lies and flattery to gain an advantage with other people. The bottom line is that people should never be more important to us than God. We must worship the Creator, not His creation.

DEFINING TRUTH:
Your ability to treat people impartially comes from your security in Christ.

PUT OFF

1. Confess it and get rid of it

Has the Holy Spirit convicted you of any areas of people-pleasing in your life? If so, write the sinful patterns you see in your life here, and ask the Lord for forgiveness.

_____

_____

2. Deal with it

Has your sin been public to the point that you need to ask someone else to forgive you? Who is that person and what is the situation?

_____

_____

3. Cut it out

What do you need to remove from your life in order to make it harder for you to commit the sin of people-pleasing? (Unhealthy friendships? Social media? Out-front ministries that tempt you to display pride?)

_____

_____

Renew Your Mind

1. Memorize it

Write out the verse that you plan to memorize.

_____

_____

_____

2. Meditate on it

How will this passage help you to please God rather than people?

_____

_____

PUT ON

1. Swap it

How are you going to please God more than pleasing people?

_____

_____

2. Check up on it

Who are you going to ask to check up on you in this struggle? When are you going to ask them?

_____

_____

Since this can often be a heart attitude, come up with a question that you want them to ask you that won't let you get away with anything.

_____

_____

11
Fearfully and Wonderfully Made

You can't have a book about defining who you are without a chapter on your physical appearance. You had to know this was coming. How does this fall under the heading of how you relate to other people? Easy. I'll bet not a day goes by that you don't think about the way you look or the way some other girl looks. The world today practically revolves around appearance. It completely affects how you view yourself, how other people view you, and how you view others.

Beautiful people are worshipped in America, and the way girls view themselves comes from what the world tells them is beautiful. To decide whether or not we're beautiful, we compare ourselves to every other girl around us, whether she's an actress, an athlete, a singer, or the girl sitting next to you in class or at church. We either feel really good about ourselves based on how *that* poor girl looks, or we feel devastated by our appearance based on how that supermodel looks.

As you've probably figured out by now, in this book we're using a different standard. Rather than "How do I feel or how do other people feel about the way I look?" we're asking "How does God feel about the way I look?" I'm sure you've heard some of these things before, but there may be a few ideas that are new to you. This isn't going to be an exhaustive look at self-esteem or body image. However, in this chapter I'm calling for a complete change of mindset that I believe could truly revolutionize the way you look at yourself and other girls for the rest of your life. Interested?

I'll start with a question that you've probably thought about and maybe even been asked: Is there anything about your body and appearance that you would change if you could? (I'm only giving you a small space, so no books, please.)

_____

_____

How often do you think about wanting to change that part of yourself?

_____

_____

What made you start thinking that this part of you was a problem? Did someone tease you about it? Do you differ from what people on TV say is beautiful? Do you have trouble finding clothes that fit?

_____

_____

I'm pretty sure most of you could fill in the blank about your worst attribute very quickly. How do I know that? Simple. You're a girl.

Picture This

I remember when I first got married. I surveyed myself in the mirror one day and listed a bunch of things I hated about myself to my husband. Michael argued with me—because he's a good husband—and said that it annoyed him how girls were always picking out their own flaws like that. I asked him what he would want to change about himself. You'd think I'd asked him to list all fifty states names backwards in alphabetical order.

Finally he said, "Uh. When I was thirteen, I thought my feet were too big, I guess. I don't know. Guys don't really think about that very much."

Can you imagine not thinking about that? I sure can't. I identified exactly what was wrong with my appearance the day I became aware that I had a body, which was at about age eleven. Turns out, guys are more on the right track (this time).

READ ALL ABOUT IT

Let's look at some verses about our creation and appearance and see what God says.

And God said, Let us make man in our image, after our likeness. . . . So God created man in his own image, in the image of God created he him; male and female created he them.

And God saw every thing that he had made, and, behold, it was very good. . . . (Genesis 1:26–27, 31)

Look up the words, *image* and *likeness* in your concordance. These words are in Hebrew, not Greek this time. What do those words mean?

image (6754)

_____

likeness (1823)

_____

What do the following verses tell you about your response to your appearance?

Woe unto him that striveth with his Maker! Let the potsherd strive with the potsherds of the earth. Shall the clay say to him that fashioneth it, What makest thou? or thy work, He hath no hands? (Isaiah 45:9)

_____

_____

Thy hands have made me and fashioned me. (Psalm 119:73)

_____

_____

For thou hast possessed my reins: thou hast covered me in my mother's womb. I will praise thee; for I am fearfully and wonderfully made: marvellous are thy works; and that my soul knoweth right well. My substance was not hid from thee, when I was made in secret, and curiously wrought in the lowest parts of the earth. (Psalm 139:13–16)

_____

_____

What are the three questions these verses ask?

Nay but, O man, who art thou that repliest against God? Shall the thing formed say to him that formed it, Why hast thou made me thus? Hath not the potter power over the clay, of the same lump to make one vessel unto honour, and another unto dishonour? (Romans 9:20–21)

_____

_____

Who is directly responsible for the specifics of your appearance?

But now, O Lord, thou art our father; we are the clay, and thou our potter; and we all are the work of thy hand. (Isaiah 64:8)

"All things" in John 1:3 includes you! Who was also involved in your creation? In other words, who is the *Him* in this verse? You may need to read John 1:1–2 for help.

All things were made by him; and without him was not any thing made that was made. (John 1:3)

The first thing you need to realize about your appearance is that God made you. I know, you already knew that, but really stop and think about it.

Picture This

My job during college was in the wig shop, meaning that I made wigs, beards, and mustaches that actors wore in plays. Making a full wig involves at least one hundred hours. We had to take the measurements of the actor's head, stuff a fake head pattern to the exact same measurements, stretch the base of the wig, which is thin netting with tiny holes called lace over the head pattern, sew darts by hand into the lace, and then take a small hooked instrument (like a slightly bent sewing needle with a handle) along with a handful of human hair and hook each individual hair into each individual lace hole—one or two hairs at a time. Let's just say, it was tedious work.

You can imagine how I felt after one hundred hours of working on the same wig, day after day, hair after hair. When it was finally finished, cut, and styled, I took pictures of it. I caught myself staring at it admiringly; I brought friends to the shop to show them; and when my wig appeared in scene one of act two of the play, I whispered to everyone I was with, "That's *my* wig. I *made* that."

If I felt that way over a clump of hair stitched into some netting, imagine how God thinks of His creation—you. Not only did He put each hair on your head, He created the hair—and your head! He carefully selected whether your nose would look like your mom's or dad's or neither of them. He determined how tall you were going to be when you reached your full height. He knew exactly what size clothes you were going to wear during your lifetime. He knew at what age you were going to get glasses or braces or struggle with acne. He picked out your exact eye color. He formed your ears to His exactly perfect specifications. Think about the word *made* in that way.

What's It Mean?

Go back through the verses above and circle every word or phrase that refers to God creating you. All of those words refer to God putting great care and love into the forming of *you*!

I especially love Psalm 139. The psalmist calls God's creation of each individual child *marvelous* or *wonderful* (extraordinary and separate). *Fearfully* means *to be in awe of*. *Wonderfully made* is my favorite phrase. It means *distinct, marked out, separate*.

This seems to be the main problem for girls today. The world has set up a specific standard for what is beautiful and perfect for a girl's appearance. If you don't weigh a certain amount, wear certain clothes, reach a certain height, have a certain face structure, or have certain parts of you enhanced, you don't meet the standard. There's something wrong with you. I saw a segment on a television show about a thirteen-year-old girl who decided to have ear-reduction surgery to avoid being teased at school. Plastic surgery is becoming the norm, not only for adults, but also for young teens who haven't even finished developing yet but have been told that they don't meet *the standard*.

Psalm 139 says that God specifically created each one of us differently . . . on purpose. God is the standard of beauty. His standard is completely different from the world's. You are marvelous, uniquely created, and awe-inspiring. Think about it. Creation is awesome. Can *you* create a person out of nothing? Me neither. But God created you and formed each little detail about you before your parents even knew you were coming into the world.

In the rest of this chapter, we're going to look at three principles that will help us change our mindset about outward appearances. First, we'll look at God's view of you; second we'll see that there's much more to you than your appearance; and third, we'll see how these principles apply, not only to your view of yourself but also your view of every other girl you'll ever come in contact with.

[DEFINING TRUTH:
God's view of your appearance is far different from the world's view.

Here's where we're going to venture into territory you might not have explored before. Remember that characteristic of yourself that you would change if you could? I want you to think about some things:

- Who told you that there was something wrong with that part of you? God? No, because He designed it that way.
- Who decided that you have to weigh a certain amount to be beautiful? God? Nope, because He created each body to carry weight differently.
- Who decided that there are certain perfect proportions for all your facial and body features? God? Can't be, since He clearly and purposefully made all different proportions.
- Who said long legs are more desirable than short legs? God? Not finding that in my Bible.

137

I would propose that beauty is all culturally determined. If you look through history, you'll discover that at one time, having pale skin was thought to be beautiful. A girl who was naturally tan was considered handicapped in the beauty department. There was a time when men looked for a lady with a double chin, as that was a sign of great beauty. At another time, plump was good, and still another time, women wore corsets because apparently, not breathing was considered fashionable. OK, maybe it was because they wanted a fifteen-inch waist. Let's not even get started on clothing and hairstyle trends! Ever look at pictures from the '80s and '90s? Yikes.

Our culture determines what is beautiful and for some reason, we poor girls just follow blindly along. But we do more than just listen to what the world says is beautiful. We have that standard so firmly set in our minds that it's how we judge ourselves and everyone around us. I think we also project that standard onto how we think God views us. I know I always have.

I've always been told that God loves me as much as He loves anyone else, like, for example, a supermodel. Yet somehow my mindset has always been that He knows deep down that He did a better job on His creation of her. I've always thought He looks down from heaven at a girl who meets the world's standard of beauty and a girl who doesn't and says, "I love you both the same even though I created one of you prettier."

Does that sound like God to you? Why or why not?

———————————————————————

———————————————————————

The more I've studied these verses about creation, the more I truly believe that's *not* how God looks at us at all! He doesn't have the same standard that the world has in any other area; why would He agree with the world about beauty? A creator doesn't usually think his creation is ugly. A creator sets out to make something beautiful, and we don't have just any creator, we have *the perfect* Creator. The world's standards change by decade or century, but God is unchangeable, so His standard never changes. I urge you to think again about that part of yourself that you hate, and ask yourself where you got the idea that there was something wrong with you. Is the answer that God told you there was something wrong with your body? I can tell you right now, it's not.

I hope we can all get this into our heads. Our culture has tried to brainwash us into thinking that there are people who are beautiful and people who aren't, and the people who aren't should do whatever they need to do to look like the people who are. The perfect Creator wasn't trying to ruin your life by giving you lots of freckles or making your hips wider than your best friend's. It's the world's confused idea that there's a right or a wrong way for a girl to look.

A big issue in our culture today is weight. Thin is in. *Thin* is too mild a word for it. *No-flab-on-any-part-of-you-anywhere-or-you-should-be-dieting-for-life* is in. Why do you think there are so many eating disorders cropping up in girls everywhere? I challenge you to find a verse that commands you to be thin. Go ahead. Look for it. The closest thing you'll probably find is that our body is the temple of the Holy Spirit, so we should take care of it. That isn't a command to be *thin*. Should you have discipline in what you eat and work to keep your body in good health so that you can serve and glorify the Lord? Yes. Does that look the same for every person? No.

You can't spend thirty minutes watching TV or browsing the Internet without seeing an ad for a fitness or weight-loss program. Our culture is obsessed with body image. Girls, you just can't get around this fact: God does not put a great emphasis on weight or looks in the Bible. He just doesn't. The world has created that standard for us, and we blindly obsess about it right along with them.

It's not just weight either: we're supposed to have perfect skin, toned legs, straight white teeth, proportional ears and nose, manicured nails, groomed eyebrows, narrow hips, curvy rear, good cleavage, slender neck, sculpted arms, and on into infinity we could go. Girls that don't measure up fall into despair and try their entire lives to correct themselves, while God looks down at His beautiful creations, saddened that they bought into the world's lies about their appearance and are wasting their time (and often lots of money) trying to fix something that doesn't need fixing!

Disclaimer: I have to put this in here. I don't want you to think that I'm advocating an undisciplined life. The Holy Spirit does live inside of us, so we should take care of our bodies to have the energy to serve and glorify Him. The Bible also talks about disciplining ourselves both physically and spiritually, so this is not a call to eat whatever you want, lie around all day, and put no effort into your appearance whatsoever. But my point is that appearance should not have the huge emphasis in our minds that it does. You understand what I'm saying. Right?

I exercised like crazy when I was a teenager. I started counting calories by the time I was thirteen. I restricted my sugar intake obsessively and watched what I ate very carefully. Some of you have never had to worry about any of that, and some of you know exactly what I'm talking about. I was constantly frustrated by the fact that many of my friends ate tons of junk food and never did a single workout, but were still way skinnier than I was and could wear anything they wanted. I remember enviously watching some older teen girls and asking a thirty-something friend how those girls could possibly be so skinny. She rolled her eyes and said, "It's called being seventeen and having a metabolism that won't quit." So I held my breath, waiting for the magical day when my metabolism would turn seventeen and not quit. Yeah, that didn't really happen for me.

Why did I go to all that trouble? I'd love to say I was disciplining myself for God's glory, but honestly I didn't give a single thought to how those things affected my ability to serve

God. I was much more worried about fitting in, looking as good as other girls, and getting praise and attention for all the wrong things.

The point is that no matter what you or I look like, we should all have the goal of disciplining ourselves and our bodies to better serve and glorify God. I recently had coffee with one of my ultra-skinny childhood friends (who used to complain about *not* being able to gain weight . . . man, I hated that), and when I ran this chapter by her, she reminded me that thin people need to take care of their bodies too. She wanted me to add that just because your outside looks the way you want it to, you don't have an excuse to eat junk food and lie around all day. Keeping the insides of our bodies healthy is important for all of us. I'm glad she said that because I probably belong to the school of thought of, "Hey, if you're skinny, by all means don't kill yourself with all that exercise." But that's the point; just wanting to look better isn't a valid goal. Glorifying God with our bodies should always be our goal.

What does God say in Genesis 1:31, when He looked at all of His creation?

_____

_____

That included Eve. We have no idea what Eve looked like. I think we all picture her as drop-dead gorgeous. Adam sure thought so. But God didn't give us her picture. For all we know, she could've been the complete opposite of what we consider beautiful today! She might've been considered overweight by today's standards; her ears might've stuck out; she might've had thick thighs or a large nose. But whatever she looked like, God looked at His creation and called her *very good*. Eve wasn't conscious of her looks or concerned about her body—that didn't come until after sin entered the world. But sin didn't change the Creator. He's still perfect and still delights in creating people who are beautiful to Him. Sin only changed the creature who suddenly started questioning why the Creator made her the way He did.

What's It Mean to You?

Don't let the world tell you that the way God made you needs to be fixed. I truly believe that most of my life, my entire mindset about appearance has been inconsistent with what I know about God and how He sees others and me. Join me in meditating on Psalm 139, and see what you come up with for yourself.

So what *should* our response be? Psalm 139:14 gives us the answer.

_____

_____

We've come back to that again, haven't we? It is never about us. Everything is about giving glory to God. If you have the kind of appearance that the world says is beautiful, praise Him, for you are fearfully and wonderfully made, but you have no reason for pride. The world's messed-up standard approves of your appearance, but that's not the point. *God* designed you exactly how He meant to, and that's what matters. Praise Him!

If you have the kind of appearance that the world ignores or even mocks, praise Him, for you are fearfully and wonderfully made, but you have no reason to hate the way you look. *God* designed you perfectly in His sight. We need a total mind overhaul on this subject.

I know this response isn't easy! In fact, sometimes it seems impossible, but please try to grasp this now. The world is a walking contradiction. Celebrities are conducting all kinds of "Celebrate You" campaigns to encourage girls to accept themselves and be confident about their appearance just the way they are. Yet the same celebrities allow their own images to be airbrushed, retouched, slimmed down, and digitally perfected when they appear on a magazine cover. Talk about mixed signals.

The world tells you that you should accept yourself and have high self-esteem.

The Bible gives you the why and the how of accepting your appearance: your loving Heavenly Father made you exactly the way you are to give Him glory.

DEFINING TRUTH:
God sees you as much more than a body.

The next point that differs from what the world says is this: your body is the least important part of you. I'm reading a book called *Done* by Cary Schmidt. In this book, he systematically shows the difference between Christianity and all other religions. One of his chapters is called "More than a Body," in which he proves that we all have souls that will live somewhere forever:

> More than a body? You bet! Your body is just a temporary dwelling place for the real you! God even calls it a "tabernacle" or a tent (2 Corinthians 5:1)! Just as you take off one set of clothes each night and put on another set the next morning, one day you will vacate your body. We call this death, which literally means "separation." Your soul will vacate its tent. In that moment, your body will cease to breathe and move and function, but the real you—the inner man—will very much continue to live!

> Yes, you are more than a body! Take care of yours while you have it, but don't focus so much on the physical that you miss "what you cannot see with your eyes!" You are soul. You have a conscience. You are created."[1]

Try to think of your body from that perspective. Your body exists to contain your soul while here on earth. That's the important part of you. Someday your earthly body will be buried and disintegrate into dust, but your soul will live forever. Kind of takes the emphasis off the physical body, doesn't it?

Look up 1 Samuel 16:7. What is the difference between how man judges and how God judges?

_____

_____

Growing up at a Christian camp, I saw lots of the same people come through year after year. When I was a very little girl whenever one of these people would tell me or my parents that I was cute, my parents would answer the same way without fail, even making me say it myself when I was a little older: "Thank you, but we're working on being pretty inside." Man, I hated that phrase! As a proud little girl, I just wanted to toss my hair, straighten my shoulders, and bask in the moment of praise. Now I understand that my parents were trying their hardest to send an early message to me: God cares about a pretty heart that wants to please Him, not a pretty face.

What's It Mean to You?

While we should seek to be good stewards of the body God gave us—since 1 Corinthians 6:19 tells us it is the temple of the Holy Spirit—our appearance is not the most important thing. When we worry about how we look, wish we looked differently, try to use our appearance to gain popularity, or flaunt our bodies immodestly to get attention from guys, we're living like a beautiful outside is the most important thing.

Here's where studying all the things we learned have about who we are in Christ comes back in. List some of the important things that we've studied about you that have nothing to do with your appearance and everything to do with being *pretty inside.*

_____

_____

God looks at your heart and sees who you are in Christ, not how gorgeous your outside is!

[**DEFINING TRUTH:**
God looks on your heart, just as He does for every girl around you.

Finally, realizing that God created each person in His own beautiful, unique, and perfect way and that your body is not the most important thing about you should affect not only how you view yourself, but also how you look at other people.

How have you recently gossiped about another girl or made fun of her appearance?

_____

_____

How have you tried harder to be nice to or friends with more attractive people?

_____

_____

What do you think could be a reason people are drawn more to attractive people? Is your reason valid in God's eyes?

_____

_____

Do you often compare your appearance with another girl's, either noticing that you look better than she does or that she's prettier than you are? Who have you compared yourself with recently?

_____

_____

With what sin(s) are you struggling if you decide that you're prettier than someone else?

_____

_____

With what sin(s) are you struggling if you're upset that someone is prettier than you?

_____

_____

Do you treat this person badly, gossip about her or think sinful thoughts about her because of your jealousy?

_____

_____

Our minds have been so influenced by the world's thinking that beauty is everything that sometimes it's very hard to remember God created *each* girl unique and beautiful in His sight, the same as He created you. When we compare our appearance with other girls', we usually come out with one of the two reactions above: pride or envy and jealousy.

Both reactions are the opposite of Christ's love. In 1 Corinthians 13 we learn that "love does not envy or boast; it is not arrogant." So both of those attitudes strike out.

What's It Mean to You?

If we believe that, by the world's standard, we are prettier than most, we are proud. And let's face it, probably all of us have found at least one person we think we're prettier than.

We already established earlier that none of us has anything to be proud about, and I hope you see from this chapter that God doesn't care about outward beauty and that He has a very different standard of beauty from what the world has pounded into our heads. God does give a very clear picture of how He views a proud person though. He says in Proverbs 16:5: "Everyone who is arrogant in heart is an abomination to the Lord; be assured, he will not go unpunished."

Look up the Hebrew word *abomination* in *Strong's* (8441). Write the definition.

_____

_____

Still feel pretty? If we're proud, we're not. God calls us disgusting. Ouch.

If we compare with others and come out believing that just about every other girl in the world is prettier than we are, we have low self-esteem . . . just kidding. (Gotcha!) That's what the world would tell us.

The fact is, we actually have high self-esteem, or to put it bluntly—we're still proud. *What?* That's right. We're thinking of only ourselves as we compare ourselves to everyone around us. When we're looking for someone over whom we can triumph by being prettier—that's pride. When we decide that we're ugly and have a pity party over the way God made us, we're focusing on ourselves—that's pride. When we're envious of another girl's appearance and want it for ourselves so that we'll get the attention she gets—that's pride too.

Envy and pride actually have a connection. It's found in Galatians 5:26: "Let us not be desirous of vain glory [conceited], provoking one another, envying one another." When we are proud and seek the praise of people, and we don't get it, we often envy. We desire the looks of another person. Why? So that we can be noticed, liked, popular, and receive the praise of people.

It's a vicious cycle really. If every girl is walking around comparing herself to every other girl, she's going to think she's prettier than some and become proud; but she will also find some that are prettier than she is, and she's going to become envious. What if we all make a conscious decision to think God's way about beauty and stop the cycle?

WRAP IT UP

If you meditate on the fact that God made each girl different and uniquely beautiful in His sight, how would that change the way you view yourself?

_____

_____

Would meditating on God's perfect creation of you encourage pride or humility in your life? Why?

_____

_____

How would it change how much time, thought, and money you spend on your outward appearance?

_____

_____

How would that change the way you view other girls' appearances?

_____

_____

How would your view about your appearance change if you meditated on the fact that your soul is eternal and that it is the most important thing about you?

_____

_____

How would that change your view about the importance of other girls' appearances?

_____

_____

How much of girls' petty arguments, gossip, mean teasing, backstabbing, cliques, bullying, cat fighting, pity parties, jealousy, favoritism, and general drama would just disappear if we had God's view of our appearances? A lot.

We're in Christ, therefore we should be like Christ. Christ is love. Love is not proud or envious.

The world is probably not going to change its emphasis on external beauty, but we Christians can. Ask God to show you how you need to change your thinking about your own appearance and about the appearance of girls around you.

DEFINING TRUTH:
Your security about your appearance is found only in Christ.

Did God reveal any sinful thoughts or actions in your life related to your appearance or other girls' appearances? What specifically?

_____

_____

PUT OFF

1. Confess it and get rid of it

What sinful thoughts about beauty have turned into sinful actions toward other girls?

_____

_____

2. Deal with it

Who do you need to ask to forgive you for the way you've treated her or talked about her, or the way you've talked about and flaunted yourself?

_____

_____

3. Cut it out

What do you need to cut out of your life to make it harder for you to continue in your sin?

_____

_____

Renew Your Mind

1. Memorize it

Write out the verse that you plan to memorize.

_____

_____

_____

2. Meditate on it

How will this passage help you focus on biblical beauty?

_____

_____

PUT ON

1. Swap it

What attitudes and actions can you put into place in your life that are the opposite of your sinful ones?

_____

_____

2. Check up on it

Who are you going to ask to keep you accountable with these struggles? For this one, maybe the best people actually would be your friends. When will you talk to one of them about helping you?

_____

_____

If you share this with them and they get it too, you can keep each other accountable when you're following the world's standard of beauty yourselves or putting down other girls' because of their appearances.

12 United with All Other Believers

amilies are complicated little units. You might think your family is the craziest one out there with its many different personalities coexisting under one roof. Every individual family, and possibly every *member* of that family, has a unique way of approaching conflict, having fun, organizing schedules, disciplining, celebrating, working, and generally making life work. Add a family reunion to the mix—a get-together of large groups of different family units all related to each other somehow or other—and you have even more diversity . . . and chaos. Family reunions are often mocked and sometimes dreaded as times of too many distinct personalities trying to peacefully make it through a day without conflict. Even in the best of families, there will be differences of opinion and little quirks that get under somebody's skin.

Picture This

Imagine the biggest family reunion to ever take place. The patriarch of the family sets the date and time, and no one else knows it. The meeting place is selected and the activities are planned. The family itself is spread across the whole world; it's so big, only a few of the family members have actually even met before. There won't be any conflict or fighting. No one will be annoyed with anyone else. There will not be gossiping, competing, or comparing. Everyone will enjoy doing the exact same thing. It's going to last a long time—forever. You are a part of this family.

Any idea what we're talking about here?

READ ALL ABOUT IT!

This huge family is Christ's family. You are related to all other believers because all of us are in Christ.

Read Galatians 3:26–29. From what we've studied before, what do the phrases "in Christ Jesus" in verse 26 and "put on Christ" in verse 27 mean?

God adopted you and made you a joint heir with Christ when you became a Christian. According to verse 26, what is true about all other Christians?

Read 1 Corinthians 1:2–3. What do these beautifully worded verses tell you about believers everywhere?

I often skim over verses like 1 Corinthians 1:2–3, those parts of Paul's opening statements that seem to have little to do with me. But look at the rich thoughts included in them: "with **all** that in **every place** call upon the name of Jesus Christ

our Lord, both **theirs and ours**: Grace be unto you, and peace, from God **our** Father, and from the Lord Jesus Christ."

In your physical family, only a few people can truly call your dad *Dad*. He is only the father of you and your siblings. You are united as a family by your parents. You have jokes that only your family understands. You have common experiences because you've shared the same life.

The same is true for you and all other believers. You now have the same Father. All of us were adopted into the same family. I love that Paul talks about grace and peace from our Father. You experience the grace and peace of God in your life, and ... guess what? ... all true believers do. Paul is bringing up a common language that all of us speak because we're family. We share the same life in Christ. All believers inherit the same blessings that you received at salvation.

Continue reading in 1 Corinthians 1 and look at verses 4–9. List some of the things we all have in common in Christ Jesus.

_____

_____

Turn to Colossians 3 and read verses 1–4 and record more of the things you share with other believers.

_____

_____

What's It Mean?

You know you're one with Christ, because you became identified with Him at salvation, but have you ever thought that every other Christian anywhere and everywhere is also one with Christ? If they're one with Christ, and you're one with Christ, you are one with *every* other believer in Christ! Whoa!

I don't know about you, but looking at believers in this light gives me a whole new perspective on how I treat them or even think about them. Look at how much you share with all believers. You share your Father and an entire spiritual life with them. You have far more important things in common with them than you have differences with them.

What's It Mean to You?

So that Christian girl in your youth group who seriously annoys you every time you see her? Yep, you're united with her in Christ.

That guy who's a little weird and everyone avoids at your Christian school? If he's a believer, you're related to him in Christ.

Your sibling who sometimes drives you up the wall? Your spiritual brother or sister.

The missionaries that spoke in church and you've never even met? They're in your family.

A believer in another country who doesn't speak your same language? You'll be spending all of eternity with them.

Being united with all believers isn't an option. We don't pick and choose with whom we're united in Christ, just like we don't pick our physical family. It's just a fact. We are all one unit in Christ! There are lots of ways this knowledge can affect our attitude toward and our interactions with other believers.

How should your unity in Christ affect what you talk about with other believers?

_____

_____

How should you treat other Christians who are different from you or might even annoy you?

_____

_____

How should you treat true believers who have different standards than you do?

_____

_____

How can our unity in Christ change the way you think about and pray for believers you've never even met?

_____

_____

How can it affect the way you talk about other believers?

_____

_____

How can you pray for other believers?

_____

_____

Anything convicting in that list? Sure was for me! If we could keep this unified, family perspective, just imagine all of the conflicts within our spiritual family that would be automatically resolved.

This knowledge could revolutionize these areas of our interaction with others and more:

- stop us from gossiping about our friends
- help us include outsiders in our groups
- motivate us to pray for missions and believers in other countries
- give us patience with other believers' faults
- stop comparing talents and criticizing or judging other Christians
- give us genuine love for our Christian family
- make us passionate about bringing lost people into this family

Someday we're going to live with these believers with the common goal of worshiping God forever. Maybe we should get a head start practicing truly unifying biblical love and setting aside sinful conflicts while here on earth.

Like I said, our unification with all other believers in Christ is a fact, but that still doesn't stop us from *acting* "disunified." It's not just, *bang*, we're saved, and suddenly we all get along perfectly. Just like your physical family can go through conflicts, our spiritual family can act divided.

Read on in 1 Corinthians 1:10–13, and you see that the Corinthian church was arguing and splitting up over a little thing like who had baptized them. To us that sounds pretty silly, but conflicts happen. Think of and write down one conflict, big or small, that you're currently involved in with another believer.

_____

_____

If I could read your answer, it might seem really pointless to me, and you'd probably think the same of the example I thought of. Or it might be a really big, hurtful issue. Paul's solution is the same for you as it was for the Corinthians in 1:10.

What was his solution, and whose name does he use to urge them to unity?

_____

_____

The unifying factor for all Christians is that Christ lives in all of us. Unity isn't something you can force, just like you can't magically conjure up biblical love without proper motivation. Unity comes when you meditate on who you are in Christ and realize that He gave all other believers the same precious promises that He's given you. And Christ, who lives in all believers, is the one who enables us to be unified as one family.

Let's look at some ways that Christ can help us to be unified. But remember, none of them can be done in your own strength. If you try to *just do* all of these things by yourself, you will fail because they sure can be hard!

Don't Judge

Read Romans 14:10–12. The Lord condemns a critical judgmental spirit of one believer toward another. In areas that aren't clearly spelled out in the Bible, standards may differ among Christians, but whose heart and life are you responsible for before God?

It's not our job to judge the motives and hearts of Christians around us. Judging simply causes division and conflict among believers and encourages pride in our own lives. Remember where all believers came from and where we're all headed. We're all sinners, equally guilty and miraculously saved by Christ, and *He* will judge everyone in heaven. We're not better than any Christian around us. In God's eyes, we're all equally justified and all equally have Christ's righteousness. We don't have a right to attack another Christian or try to judge her heart. Even when a believer is sinning, it's not our job to condemn her, talk about her sin to others, or look down on her. But that being said, go on to the next point.

Lovingly Confront Sin

Believe it or not, this actually encourages unity. Even though most of us would love to avoid confrontation at all costs, Galatians 6:1 says, "Brethren, if a man be overtaken in a fault, ye which are spiritual, restore such an one in the spirit of meekness; considering thyself, lest thou also be tempted." When we *do* see sin in a fellow Christian's life, we're not to gossip about it, condemn them as hopeless, or look down on them in pride. *You who are spiritual* doesn't mean "you who are better than they are." It means "you who are walking according to the Holy Spirit" and "you who are more spiritually mature in that area." *Restore* means to "repair them or make them useful" to the body of Christ again. *Gentleness* means "humility." Why should we be humble when dealing with sin, according to the rest of the verse?

_____

_____

Confronting our friends' sin God's way will bring unity because it helps a sister get back on track to serving the Lord. It also reminds us that we're not above anyone else's sin. We could each become involved in our own sin at any time, and we may need another Christian to come help us. When confrontation is handled in a spirit of humility, it increases Christian fellowship and reminds us that we're all just sinners, striving for the same goal of glorifying God with our lives.

Don't Argue, Forgive

Colossians 3:13 holds a key to unity: when someone has wronged us, instead of arguing or holding it against them, we forbear and forgive. Here's one of the coolest definitions ever: *forbear* means *to put up with*. We can't allow a conflict with a believer to break the unity we all have in Christ. We shouldn't get impatient with them, but rather should *put up with* them. Then we should *forgive*, which means *to be gracious, kind and benevolent, and to deliver them from our debt*, even when they don't deserve it. We're not to get bitter, hold it over their heads, or keep the conflict going, no matter how hurtful it was. According to Colossians 3:13, what is the motivation for and the only way that we can give this forgiveness?

_____

_____

When we're all fully aware of the great debt Christ forgave us, it's a lot harder to refuse to give the same forgiveness to a person who also shares in Christ's abundant love and forgiveness. Easier said than done, right? That's why we can't just decide to forgive someone in our own strength. It has to come from understanding the forgiveness and love we have in Christ.

Use Your Individual Gifts

Read Romans 12:4–8, and see that God gave each one of us different personalities, talents, and gifts. We're all one body, but we're different parts of the body and have different purposes to fill. The church needs each one of us to use our different strengths to serve. Even if you're still a very young lady, you can help unify the body of Christ by using your unique talents.

That being said, we shouldn't compare our gifts with others'. We shouldn't wish we could play the piano or sing if our talents are better used for serving with children. We shouldn't compare personalities and wish that we could lead publicly the way some do if we have a more behind-the-scenes serving gift. We can help to unify other believers by serving wherever we can and rejoicing that the Lord specifically gifted us the way He has to help bring unity to His body of believers.

What are some gifts you have that you could use to minister to other believers, both in church and outside of church?

_____

_____

Put On Christ

I know. That's a blanket statement. Go back to Colossians 3 and read verses 12–17, and then make a list of all the characteristics we are to put on.

_____

_____

As verse 12 says, believers—God's chosen ones—should have these traits in their lives. If all of us had these characteristics, disunity would practically disappear. Verse 15 says to allow "the peace of Christ" to "rule in your hearts."

We looked at this in Chapter 6 on reconciliation. *Peace* means *to set at one again*. When we love others the way Christ loved us, we will be unified through Him. Just like always, Scripture comes back to Christ in verse 17, saying simply that we're to do everything in the name of Christ, which will bring God glory. This is the purpose of all Christians. We should all be unified around this common goal of bringing God glory, and we should be passionate about loving each other enough to help each other reach this all-important end.

WRAP IT UP

When we ask the teens in our youth group what spiritual quality they're working on, they say things like being kind or patient. That's often the same thing many of us struggle with on a day-to-day basis: relating to people in a Christ-honoring way. And this is why knowing our position with Christ and realizing that every believer around us is also *in Christ* can change the way we interact with people.

We won't be quick to judge because we know how sinful we are ourselves. We won't argue or hold grudges because we know that we share the same Lord as this person and that He has forgiven this person far more than we could ever forgive. We'll be humble when confronting sin because we know how wicked our own hearts are. We may even be more open to talking about our sin struggles with others because we're humble enough to seek their help and encouragement, without worrying that they'll judge us. We speak the same language as our spiritual family. We'll be able to love each other supernaturally, because all believers have experienced Christ's supernatural love.

Colossians 3:11 sums up this whole chapter on unity in the last seven words of the verse. This is true of all Christians. Write the phrase here.

_____

_____

Try to view all believers around you as being in Christ, just as you are, and see how that affects the way you treat them.

Identify the areas in your life in which you are sinning in your thoughts about and actions toward other believers. Ask the Lord to forgive you for your disobedience to His direct command to be unified.

_____

_____

> **DEFINING TRUTH:**
> Your relationship with all other believers is defined in Christ.

PUT OFF

1. Confess it and get rid of it

Are you using the gifts the Lord gave you to serve other Christians, or are you always comparing, wishing you had different talents?

_____

_____

2. Deal with it

From which Christian sisters or brothers do you need to seek forgiveness? How can you work on your relationship with each of these people? (I doubt all of your problems with people have been just thoughts!)

_____

_____

3. Cut it out

What do you need to cut out of your life to lessen your struggle of showing Christian love to your fellow believers?

_____

_____

Renew Your Mind

1. Memorize it

Write out the verse that you plan to memorize.

_____

_____

_____

2. Meditate on it

How will this passage help you to pursue unity with other Christians?

_____

_____

_____

PUT ON

1. Swap it

Identify areas of Christian disunity in your life, whether it's in your youth group, your school, your group of friends, your family, or your workplace. Tell how you can help to encourage unity among believers in these areas.

_____

_____

2. Check up on it

Who will you ask to keep you accountable about the way you think about believers, treat believers, and use your gifts to unify the body of Christ? And when will you ask them to help you?

_____

_____

Conclusion

There's an ice cream shop close to where I live that has about fifteen machines of frozen yogurt and soft-serve ice cream. They put out enormous bowls for you to serve yourself, but they charge you by the ounce, not the size of the bowl. Before you commit to a huge bowl of a certain flavor, they give you tiny sample cups to try a taste. If you like it (hello, triple chocolate cheesecake!), you can get as much as you want . . . or at least as much as you're prepared to pay for.

At this point in our study, you may be feeling like I just dumped a boatload of truth on you and you're struggling to absorb so many verses and big concepts about the gospel and what it means to be in Christ. Guess what? That was a teeny tiny sample cup, barely enough to even taste. My goal is to whet your appetite, so that you'll say, "That's amazing! I need a big bowl of that." The Bible is an endless buffet of incredibly rich truths. You can go back for more your entire life and never get enough of it.

This Bible study includes only a few of my favorite passages from my study of the topic. Girls, you have a whole lifetime to dig into this on your own and discover deeper levels of Christ's riches. Please don't be satisfied by the sample cups you can get from a book or from a message. Now that you have a small taste of some of the things Christ has done for you, what do you do with this knowledge? You have to apply it, or you'll just forget everything you studied and go on living as before.

I hope you can see how these incredible principles relate to your everyday life. The Bible has the answer for every insecurity you will ever face. Don't listen to the world's answers. Don't depend on yourself or look to others for affirmation. Don't define yourself based on what's popular or what feels right at the time.

Define yourself by Christ. Only then will you truly be secure and free to be exactly who God says you are.

Appendix 1

PUT OFF, RENEW, PUT ON

Welcome, Chapter 1 readers! Way to follow instructions. Ten points for you.

We're going to use Ephesians 4:22–24 a lot to apply the truth of each lesson. You'll be identifying certain sins in your life. But that's only the first step. You actually have to deal with the sin, or you'll keep doing it forever, and you'll never change and grow. Ephesians 4 gives three principles to use when dealing with our sinful hearts, and each one has several steps. Let's break them down.

First, we have to put off the sin. Our youth group did an activity called Nasty Night, which involved the grossest things we youth leaders could dream up. A ketchup and syrup filled water balloon fight; fishing marbles out of a pool of baked beans with our toes; sorting through a big, messy vat of SpaghettiOs to spell out words. By the end of the night we were all unrecognizable, coated with sticky condiments and gummy flour from our hair to our toes. We couldn't wait to just get home and take those disgusting, smelly clothes off (and possibly burn them)!

It's the same way with our sin. Once we see our stinky-idol-atrous-self-glorifying-people-worshipping ways, why would we want to do anything but get them as far away from us as possible? So just like verse 22 says, we should put it off! Get rid of it. The sins you list in each lesson are your *put offs*.

Here are the steps that fall under the **Put Off** process.

1. Confess it and get rid of it. First, you have to acknowledge your sin, agree with God that it is sin, and then get as far away from it as possible. Proverbs 28:13 says, "Whoever conceals his transgressions will not prosper, but he who confesses and forsakes them will obtain mercy."

If you see an area of sin in your life and ask the Lord's forgiveness for it, but then turn around and continue to do it, you've confessed it, but you haven't forsaken it. It's easy to just ask the Lord to forgive you for something, but to give it up can be much harder. That's the sign that you've truly seen how terrible your sin is—when you sincerely ask forgiveness and sincerely work to get it out of your life. That doesn't mean you'll never commit the sin again. You may always struggle with it, but a repentant heart will not be able to continue in the sin for very long.

2. Deal with it. Ask yourself if there is anyone other than God against whom you've sinned and from whom you need to ask forgiveness? With the confess step above, you've already asked God for forgiveness. So if your sin was a heart attitude or a thought only, then you probably don't need to ask forgiveness of a person. But, for example, if your sin was bitterness and you've hated a person, even just in your heart, you'll probably need to ask their forgiveness as well. And for any sin that affected other people, you'll need to include this step.

3. Cut it out. The clearest example I can think of to illustrate this is of extreme outdoorsman Aron Ralston. His autobiography, *Between a Rock and Hard Place*, tells his story of falling in a Utah canyon while hiking and being pinned against the canyon wall by a loose boulder. After days without help, Ralston assumes he is going to die alone in the canyon, but he summons the incredible will to free himself by breaking his own arm and amputating it using a dull knife. Honestly, I think I would've just allowed myself to die out there. I can't imagine the pain of operating on myself without even the proper tools. This is the idea of incredibly extreme amputation in a physical sense.

We're using amputation in the spiritual sense of cutting something out of your life, no matter how hard it is. In Matthew 5:28–30, Jesus gives the command to cut out your eye or cut off your hand if it causes you to sin. Christ didn't mean for everyone to do this literally. He was giving us a principle. Speaker Rand Hummel often says it this way: "Make it hard to sin and easy to do right."[1] If there is a friend who is constantly tempting you to sin when you're around them, you may have to apply the cut it off principle. Cut off your friend's hand? Of course not. But you may have to confront them, and if they refuse to change, quit hanging out with them. Maybe you struggle with gossiping every time you go on social media. (You don't have to actually talk to be gossiping; it can be done through texting or messaging too!) Maybe you need to delete your social media account. Does that sound a little extreme? Sure, but you need to ask if you love God and hate your sin enough to do whatever you need to do to stop sinning.

Our second principle is found in Ephesians 4:23— renew your mind. Hm. That one sounds a little harder, doesn't it? That's because it is, but you can't just skip this and move on to the last one. Your thinking/your heart is what determines how you sin.

To me, this is like the long, hot shower that comes after Nasty Night. You've already seen your gross, disgusting sin, and now you're ready to deal with it. You can't just use a slightly damp rag and wipe off the remaining clumps of mustard, flour, and syrup, or run your fingers through your gunked-up hair and call it a day. If you do that, when you wake up in the morning, the same nastiness would still be all over your skin and hair, not to mention that you would probably smell even worse and have attracted every bug within one hundred miles during the night! You have to thoroughly cleanse yourself. It took more than one shower and hair washing for all of the Nasty Night participants to actually feel clean. Renewing your mind will require the washing of your heart by God's Word! This is where true change actually comes about.

The two steps that go along with renewing your mind relate to God's Word.

1. Memorize it. This is a hard one for me, I'll admit. I can actually memorize things pretty easily, but disciplining myself to just do it is where I tend to struggle. But it's so important. Once you've identified your sin, you need to have verses at the ready to fight it. You can't always grab your Bible when you're tempted to think a jealous thought of a girl at school, but you can have that verse tucked away in your mind to combat that sin. Even if you have your Bible with you or have access to a Bible app on your phone, you have to know where the verse is before it can help you.

2. Meditate on it. This means to think about it. This one is especially hard these days. With the advancement of technology, we can literally have *noise* going on at all times. We have handheld devices, TVs, gaming systems, texting, instant messaging, social media, or all of them going on at once. It's hard for us to sometimes just turn everything off so we can actually think about something! If we don't though, we'll never let the truths we study and memorize burrow deep into our hearts. This is where change really happens—when we allow God to work in our hearts by turning His actual Words and truths about Him over and over in our minds. This takes time. Often we read the Bible for a few minutes and then rush on with our lives, never allowing what we read to go through our minds the rest of the day. Don't skip this step! Shut out the noise, take the time, and meditate!

Here's a quick review.

1. Put off—confess it, get rid of it, deal with it, cut it out

2. Renew your mind—memorize and mediate on God's words

And lastly . . . put on. After that luxurious shower, how ridiculous would it be for me to put those Nasty Night mustard-soaked-syrup-sticky-flour-caked clothes on again and go out shopping? Bleh. No thanks! It makes me feel sticky just thinking about it. You want to put on something clean and different. We have to put on the opposite of what we were wearing.

1. Swap it. Put on the opposite. If you continue reading in Ephesians 4 after the verses we're using, God gives us examples to illustrate the swap-it principle. In 4:25–32, you'll see examples of what to *put off*, but each one has a *put on* right after it. God doesn't just say *don't lie*, He also says *speak truth*. He not only says *don't steal*, but also *get a job* so you can give to others. He says *don't say bad things*, but also *use your words to build* people up. *Put off* bitterness and anger and gossip, and *put on* kindness. Isn't God good to give us examples?

You have to identify what your sin is but also identify with what godly action you need to replace it. You can't just pick off the bad fruit on a tree and expect good fruit to replace it. If your roots (your heart) are still corrupted, your fruit (actions, words) will still be sinful. That's why the other steps *must* come first.

2. Check up on it. Pick a person who is stronger than you are in your area of sin, and ask them to check up on you. This is where our pride comes back into play. It's hard to admit to someone that you have a sin struggle and need help. None of us naturally like to admit we're weak. This step is important because it not only keeps us humble, but it also helps us stay on the right track. If you struggle with having your devotions on a daily basis, get someone you respect to ask you if you're having your time with the Lord consistently. This could be a friend, but it's usually better to get someone in authority over you or older than you. You could have an accountability partner with a friend too, but sometimes friends cave to peer pressure and don't want to tell you the truth because they're afraid of how you'll react. (It's that old people-pleasing thing again!) Find someone who is spiritually strong, *who will commit to pray for you*, can help you when you fail, and who'll tell you the truth you need to hear.

One last thing. Ephesians 4:22–24 is part of a larger sentence that starts back in verse 20. Verses 17–19 tell the believers at Ephesus not to live just like the Gentiles do, consumed with wickedness and vain thinking. Why? Because "that is not the way you learned Christ" (4:20).

We're to put off, renew, and put on because *this is how Christ wants us to live and empowers us to live now that we belong to Him!* This is the motivation. Without the motivation of wanting to live the right way because this fits with our knowledge of Christ, even this change process can become a way to look good on the outside.

We may be tempted to skip the *renew our mind* part, because it's too hard; sometimes we will want to skip the *put off* part because we don't really want to totally give up our sin. We just skip straight to the *put on* part because that's the only part people can see, and life just works better if we look like we're good little girls doing all the right things. That's not true change, and it's not consistent with what we're going to learn about Christ.

Are you completely overwhelmed? I hope not. These are the basic steps for change that need to take place in your life for the rest of your life! If you can learn this now, you'll be way ahead of a lot of adults. This is God's plan, not mine or anyone else's. This is the only way to see real growth in your life. I didn't promise it would be easy, but keep working. Here are the steps that we'll use at the end of each lesson.

1. **Put off:** Confess it, get rid of it, deal with it, cut it out

2. **Renew your mind:** Memorize it and meditate on it

3. **Put on:** Swap it and check up on it

Now go on back to the lesson you're working on and answer the questions honestly so you can start changing God's way!

Appendix 2
Think About It

The concept of meditating on God and His words may be new to you, so I've listed a variety of sources and ideas to get you started.

- Read from a book of published prayers like *Valley of Vision* or devotional thoughts like *Morning and Evening* by Charles Haddon Spurgeon. You might find these books in a library, but you can order copies through online booksellers. Although the older language in these books may be challenging, there is much to consider and include in your prayers.

- Read, sing, or meditate on songs about your amazing salvation and redemption. Pay special attention to any times those two words are mentioned. Concentrate on what they mean. Good songs can be a great way to offer a prayer of praise to God.

- Read the lyrics from songs that focus on your guilt without Christ and your freedom from sin in Christ. Notice the vivid word pictures that contrast your heavy guilt with God's triumphant grace. You can use this as a prayer to God to thank Him for His gracious gift of freeing you from the power of sin and guilt, or use it to reinforce in your heart His promises to remove your guilt.

- Read the lyrics from songs that present the Lord as your best Friend, and think about the work Jesus did on the cross for you so you can call yourself His friend. If it weren't for Christ, we would still be His enemies!
- Read Psalm 103 and look for all of the blessings recorded. Read each blessing slowly (underline or circle each one if it will make you think about it more) and rejoice in how incredibly rich you are, daughter of God!
- Read Amy Carmichael's book *If* and meditate on what you really know about Calvary love.
- Study Matthew 6:1–18 and examine your heart. Ask yourself if you're a hypocrite. Do you seek the praise of others rather than the praise of God?
- For one week, make a concentrated effort to meditate on the principles discussed in one of these lessons. Make a conscious effort to catch yourself every time you're thinking or acting in a way that is opposed to these principles, whether it's in relation to yourself or other girls. Maybe even keep a journal of all the times you catch yourself thinking or acting unbiblically. You'll be amazed how many times our wrong thinking comes into play in everyday life.
- Meditate on Psalm 139:13–16 and ask God to change your mind about your perception of beauty.

Endnotes

INTRODUCTION

1. Examples of online resources available at the time of the publication of *I.D.: Who Am I in Christ?*: http://www.e-sword.net/; http://www.biblestudytools.com/concordances/strongs-exhaustive-concordance/; or http://www.blueletterbible.org/.

CHAPTER 1

1. Jerry Bridges, *Respectable Sins* (Colorado Springs: NavPress, 2007), 21.

2. Ibid., 29–30.

CHAPTER 2

1. Jonathan Edwards, *Sinners in the Hands of an Angry God* (New Kensington, PA: Whitaker House, 1997), 21–22.

2. Dictionary.com, s.v. "slave," accessed April 26, 2012, http://dictionary.reference.com/browse/slave.

CHAPTER 3

1. John MacArthur, *Ephesians* (Chicago: Moody Press, 1986), 24.

2. Elyse M. Fitzpatrick, *Because He Loves Me,* (Wheaton:

Crossway, 2008), 73.

CHAPTER 4
1. John MacArthur, *The MacArthur New Testament Commentary* (Nashville: Thomas Nelson, Inc., 2007), 444.

CHAPTER 5
1. Dictionary.com, s.v. "guilt," accessed April 26, 2012, http://dictionary.reference.com/browse/guilt.

CHAPTER 6
1. Milton Vincent, *A Gospel Primer for Christians* (Bemidji, MN: Focus Publishing, 2008), 91–93.

2. John MacArthur, *Ephesians* (Chicago: Moody Press, 1986), 23.

CHAPTER 8
1. Elyse M. Fitzpatrick, *Because He Loves Me* (Wheaton: Crossway, 2008), 74.

2. Ibid.

CHAPTER 9
1. John MacArthur, *Ephesians* (Chicago: Moody Press, 1986), 63.

CHAPTER 10
1. Matthew Henry, *Matthew Henry's Commentary* (Peabody, MA: Hendrickson Publishing, 1991), 6:55.

CHAPTER 11
1. Cary Schmidt, *Done* (Lancaster, CA: Striving Together Publications, 2005), 7.

APPENDIX 1
1. Rand Hummel, "Make it Hard to Sin and Easy to do Right," *Pure Truth Conference* (article). http://30daychallenge111.com/articles-2/make-it-hard-to-sin-and-easy-to-do-right/.